COME BLOW YOUR MIND WITH ME

Andrew M. Greeley

COME
BLOW YOUR MIND
WITH ME

DOUBLEDAY & COMPANY, INC. GARDEN CITY, NEW YORK
1971

Library of Congress Catalog Card Number 73–139026
Copyright © 1971 by Andrew M. Greeley
All Rights Reserved
Printed in the United States of America

Dedicated to
Cletus F. O'Donnell
Bishop of Madison, Wisconsin

Contents

Introduction

PART I

Religion in America

PART II

American Catholicism

Introduction

This book of essays is concerned with "mind blowing" in two senses:
Many of the chapters deal with the romanticism that swept through the American Church and indeed the whole American society in the last half of the 1950s, a romanticism that has increasingly become not merely anti-intellectual but irrational.

I shall make no pretense in the volume of attempting to avoid expressing my own emotional responses to the new romanticism. We are told that it is important now not so much to describe things as they are, as to describe the way we feel. I will yield at least this much to the mind blowers. There will be little doubt in their mind, when I am finished, as to how I feel.

As I hope I make clear in the title chapter, my primary emotional response to the new romanticism is one of ambivalence. Like most Irishmen, even like most attenuated Irishmen (who are called Irish-Americans), I am at heart a romantic. I am profoundly skeptical of narrow, juridic rationalism wherever it manifests itself, be it either in naive, empirical science or in naive Christianity. Christianity without emotion and feeling is a perverted Christianity, just as science without emotion and feeling is a half-blind science. On the other hand, "mind blowing," the anti-intellectualism, not to say irrationalism, of the current romantic binge, is profoundly disturbing to me. I think it is a good thing to let out the daemon within us, especially because the daemon is also a Ghost and a Spirit, but when man's rationality abdicates, his authentic daemon departs also, and what one has is not the daemonic, but all too frequently, the diabolic.

Thus I found myself in the first half of the 1960s arguing with the younger Harvey Cox that man has profound needs for the transcendent, the mythological, and the sacred, and I now find myself arguing with a more mature Cox that there must be some kind of cognitive "meaning core," other than the transcendental, for which man is searching. I agree completely with Professor Cox: man must celebrate, he must engage in festivity and fantasy, but I would add that he celebrates not simply because celebration is a good thing and because it's fun to celebrate, but rather that man celebrates because he has *reason* to celebrate. I am in sympathy with much of the theology of play, but I do not think Professor Cox or his associates in play theology have yet got around to telling us what the reasons for our celebration are. I suspect that the Dionysian turn both in the church and the larger society has the same motivation as did the Dionysian quest for ecstasy in ancient Greece—an escape from tragedy that is too much to bear, a running away from ugliness that is too horrendous to face. If mind blowing is essentially escapist—and I suspect that it is increasingly becoming that—then I want no part of it.

I do not think there is any inconsistency in my defending the mythological and the sacral against the earlier Cox and the rational and the meaningful against the later Cox. It seems to me that in both cases I am being little more than a good sociologist, a good disciple of Max Weber. I am convinced that meaning must be expressed in myth and that myths without meaning are empty and worthless. These twin convictions, I suppose, set the framework and the perspective for this book.

Heaven knows, there is ample reason for mind blowing in American Catholicism (a romanticism that Professor Philip Gleason anticipated, it seems, almost a decade ago). The narrow, juridic, rationalistic inhumanity of the petrified post-Tridentine Church in which most of us were raised kept so much that was authentically human pent up inside us that it was inevitable that once we were permitted to have emotions again we would go on a binge. Furthermore, the incredible mess made of the post-Vatican renewal during the past five years (as recorded in the four chapters of this book that were originally given as the Thomas More Lectures at Yale in 1970) is quite enough to make anybody want to get higher than a kite. Even now, one finds it very difficult to believe that all the good will and hopefulness of the early sessions of the Council could be so completely dissipated. The Pope, the Curia, and many of the bishops could not have done a better job of destroying the hopeful, positive forces that were latent in the American Church in the early 1960s if they had deliberately set out to do so.

But irrationality is not an appropriate response to frustration and disappointment, though it is certainly an understandable one. It is five years since the last collection of my occasional essays was published (*The Hesitant Pilgrim*). No one in his right mind would suggest that it has been a particularly cheerful five years. The ugly, evil, stupid Vietnamese war has corroded American society. Young and old, rich and poor, black and white, well educated and less well educated, have been set one against the other, and some political leaders are only too willing to exploit this polarization. The arrogance of the military has only been matched by the arrogance of the intellectuals and of the ignorant, fascist toughs who have anointed themselves and have been accepted as the spokesmen for the younger generation. The great leaders have all been killed or discredited, and one is faced with the chilling thought that if another great leader should appear, he, too, would be killed. The leaders we have are perhaps well meaning but plainly incapable of generating the enthusiasm and the commitment necessary to bind up the wounds of society. I am not one of those who think the United States of America is going to collapse, or even that it is in its worst crisis since the Civil War. We probably will blunder through this one and come out scarred and scathed, but still, somehow or other, we will survive. But what a futile half decade it has been.

In the American Church things are, if possible, even worse. The encyclical letter *Humanae Vitae* was an absolute disaster for the Church and for the Papacy. It is a disaster not merely because of the decision it rendered (a decision that will certainly be reversed at some time in the not too distant future), but also a disaster because it refused to take seriously the problems of population and sexuality, which are associated with birth control, or the doctrine of collegiality propounded at the Council. The Pope did not respond seriously to those critical issues that underlie the whole birth control controversy, and he did not consult with the bishops of the world in any meaningful fashion. The encyclical, as is generally well known, has been counterproductive. It has turned a considerable number of priests and lay people against the official Church position, and it would appear that, in the United States, somewhere between two thirds and three quarters of the priests and laity under forty simply reject the papal position. The American hierarchy, while it endorsed the encyclical, made little attempt to insist that it be enforced, and stood by in embarrassed silence when faced with the one situation in which a bishop had attempted to enforce it. The encylical was not then so much a disaster for the laity and the clergy as it was for the credibility of the Pope and the hierarchy; nevertheless, the Pope's decision, however well intentioned, to remove the question of sexuality from collegial discussion in the post-Vatican Church, has had a corrosive effect in the Church analogous to the impact of the Vietnam war on the rest of the society.

Furthermore, the American hierarchy seems completely lacking in effective leadership—with one or two notable exceptions. As a matter of fact, save for the well-known exceptions, one could say that the leadership in the hierarchy has probably never been worse since 1820. American Catholics have watched in shocked disbelief during the past half decade as the major sees in the country are filled, one by one, with men who do not understand the forces that the Vatican

Council has released and do in fact seem bent on action that will destroy what little credibility and effectiveness the hierarchy still enjoys. The lower clergy, to whom one would have hoped to turn for leadership in time of crisis, has turned in on itself and is trapped in a massive identity crisis. In some dioceses and religious communities, the exodus seems to have reached almost panic proportions, and as we note in chapter 8, even more serious is the virtual drying up of the vocations to the priesthood and the religious life. In *The Hesitant Pilgrim* I was cautiously hopeful about the capacity of American Catholicism to weather the post-Vatican crisis and indeed to turn the transitional era into a period of great growth. It is now, I think, perfectly clear that I was wrong. If Cardinal Meyer had lived, if *Humanae Vitae* had not been written, if, if, if. At all the critical points, all the wrong things seem to have happened. So I can understand "mind blowing," even if I do not approve of it. If ideas fail to persuade the intransigent reactionaries who hold power, of the need for change, it is easy to despair of ideas; if structures impede what one is firmly convinced is the thrust of the spirit, then it is very easy to give up on structures. The "mind blower" has done both, and he feels very good about it. It apparently has not occurred to him that social change takes place only when new directions are created and new ideas are finally accepted.

But one does not engage in argument with the "mind blowers." Shortly after the publication of "The First Papal Press Conference," two priests wrote me to say they saw through my clever ploy. All I was trying to do was to preserve "structures" in the Church under a different guise. These two simple-minded souls were completely persuaded that once they had used the evil word "structure," they had disposed of me. Structures were bad, and that was that. Their reaction was, I think, the essence of mind blowing. They did not attempt to respond to the implicit argument in "The First Papal Press Conference." They certainly were not interested in the obvious sociological fact that you do not have a society without routinized patterns of behavior (which is all that a structure is). They knew what they *felt*, and that was the end of the conversation.

The failures of Church officialdom have created the atmosphere in which the mind blowers can flourish; the failure of the former during the past five years has produced the excesses of the other, but of the two, the mind blowers are the more dangerous. The present generation of ecclesiastical leadership is living on borrowed time. No one takes it seriously any more, but the pentecostals, the cursilloists, and the sensitivity nuts are taken very seriously indeed. The intransigent immobilism of some of the hierarchy represents now nothing but themselves and the dying past. The mind blowers, I fear, could easily represent the future, and I very much doubt that it would be an improvement.

In any situation in which the context is set by the mind-blowing romanticists on the one hand and hierarchal reactionaries on the other, a number of us are going to find ourselves sitting on the sidelines. The essays will please neither the supporters of Daniel Berrigan nor those of James Francis McIntyre; however, I suspect there is a rather considerable number of people still occupying the area between these two extremes. It is for this beleaguered middle group, which I still think is a majority, that these essays are intended. The dust will finally settle someday, and that day will belong to us.

Chapter 8 was originally presented as the Thomas More Lectures at Yale University during the academic year 1969–70. I am grateful to Father Richard R. Russell for inviting me. Chapter 10 was my presidential address to the American Catholic Sociological Society. I want to take this opportunity to express my gratitude to my colleagues for bestowing that honor upon me.

PART I
Religion in America

1. Come Blow Your Mind with Me

Now we have the pot Mass.

In most respects, it's indistinguishable from any other liturgical happening to be found in the American Church. Homemade posters or banners are on the wall; the kitchen table has been converted into an altar; the priest wears a sport shirt, and some of the nuns present wear bermuda shorts; the Epistle is a passage from *The New York Times Magazine*; the Gospel is taken from the writings of Daniel Berrigan, with bongo drums beating in the background; a Beatle song serves as an Introit, and perhaps a partially clad dancer will cavort about at the Offertory. The only real difference is that, in a pot Mass, after the Homily is over some of the congregation light a marijuana cigarette—to help the charisma.

You say that I must be joking? We should be so lucky.

Marijuana liturgy is but the latest (and not necessarily the most absurd) manifestation of the fact that the American Catholic Church is going through a colossal "mind blowing" experience. It is safe to bet that something worse than the pot Mass will happen. In fact, it probably already has.

The cursillos are now something "old hat," but that peculiar combination of emotionalism, manipulation, and Falangist authoritarianism still survives. The melodies of *De Colores* still can be heard, and little groups of cursillo enthusiasts persist in bringing "love and affection" to other members of their parishes—whether these members want it or not.

Catholic pentecostalism has spread about the country, and Newman clubs are beginning to underwrite the speaking of tongues on the college campus. Perhaps this is a sort of a Catholic counterpart to astrology and witchcraft. In one recent pentecostal publication, a "witness bearer" tells how the Holy Spirit drove the devil out of him; when the devil left, he could actually smell the sulphur and brimstone, as could everyone else in the room. Other pentecostals vie with each other to speak in the most esoteric of foreign languages, including Hebrew (when there happens to be a scripture scholar present who can understand Hebrew). Indeed, one pentecostal was absolutely convinced that she was speaking Japanese, although, so far, she hasn't found anyone who understands the language to interpret what the message is.

Hordes of do-it-yourself therapists schooled in a weekend or two weeks of sensitivity training are going about the land preaching their gospel of group mental health to all that will hear, and to a good many who are not particularly interested in hearing. High schools, colleges, seminaries, novitiates, discussion groups, chapters of religious communities—no one is safe from the sensitivity cultist. In one instance I know of, a group of nuns, deeply moved by the profound openness and honesty of a sensitivity experience, sped from room to room in a convent one night, clad in the totally altogether to bring the gospel of openness and trust to their colleagues.

As Catholics become more and more aware of the refined developments of group dynamics as practiced in marathon weekends, encounter groups, Esalen groups, or even the most recent glorious innovation, "nude marathons," the sensitivity cult grows more bizarre. Dan Sullivan, the famous Catholic expert on sex—who was once described as the only man alive who could make sex sound dull—advertises in the *National Catholic Reporter* the possibility of Esalen-type encounter sessions for interested readers of that worthy journal. One would dearly love to know whether Mr. Sullivan's encounterists wear their clothes or not. But then, given the kind of person who would respond to such an advertisement in the *National Catholic Reporter*, it may not much matter.

High club dances are run for priests and nuns at summer institutes. They may not be called "high club dances," but they are, just the same, and the adolescent behavior of the participants doesn't leave much doubt. In some summer institutes, the first week is known as POW week—that is to say, "pair-off" week; everyone who is interested chooses a partner for a summer of open, honest, trusting encounter.

One no longer dares to argue from tradition, for the traditional ways were far too dry, dull, arid, and rationalistic. Authority is quite irrelevant, and there is nothing worse than being irrelevant. As a matter of fact, the only real function authority serves—at least for the mind blowers—is to provide new challenges and rules to break. As one clergyman put it, "Who is the Bishop or even the Pope to tell me how I should say Mass?"

Obviously, structures "must go"—not old, worn-out, obsolete structures, but all structures—because structures inhibit the spontaneity of the spirit. The small, informal group is the only kind of relationship that is permitted for human beings and for Christians, and within that group there must be as little differentiation in roles as is possible. In one such group that I know of, all the members of the congregation say the words of Consecration together to symbolize that no one dares to distinguish himself over against the rest of the Eucharistic community.

Nor is there any objective ethical order. A man may betray his friends, dishonor his commitments, abandon his responsibilities, desert his family, break his promises, and renege on his commitments— it doesn't matter, so long as he is "doing his own thing" and he is "sincere." In fact, there is no objective order at all, and while the military-industrial complex is evil (and, of course, so are the Hierarchy and Mayor Daley), virtually no one else is to be considered at all accountable for his behavior; so long as one asserts that one is being sincere and is maintaining one's own integrity, one can do pretty much what one pleases and even demand that one be praised for so doing.

Shocking other people is important. One denounces the Pope from the pulpit, or announces that one is about to get married. One performs invalid or sacrilegious marriage ceremonies. One teaches students that premarital sex is not only not wrong, but may even be praiseworthy. One openly defies rules and announces that a public liturgical ceremony is certainly going to lead to ecclesiastical repression (even though it turns out that it does not). One invites the members of the congregation to sip, dip, or skip.

Finally, theology is finished. Some of the mind blowers may occasionally quote a theologian—usually out of context—to justify the behavior they are engaged in, but when one responds in an attempt at serious discussion of a theologian's thought, one is told, "I don't care what Hans Küng says about the priesthood—I know what I feel about my priesthood," or "What Yves Congar thinks about the Church doesn't matter; I know when I *feel* that I'm part of the Church," or "It is completely irrelevant whether Karl Rahner says the Church has to have structure if it is to be the Church of Christ. I *know* the Church doesn't need a structure."

Aren't we all having great fun?

The trouble with much of this mind-blowing enthusiasm is that in the midst of all the lunacy, the enthusiasts make several good points, but they're made in such a context of irrationality that sane men (and one presumes there are some of them left) are apt to miss the truth that the young enthusiasts do have. Gilbert Chesterton once said that a heretic is a man who has part of the truth and thinks it is the whole truth. Alas, American Catholicism today abounds with Chestertonian heretics.

Liturgy should be a joyous celebration. Human emotions should be involved in worship, but there is something profoundly wrong with us if we need narcotics to be able to rejoice at the sacred mysteries. St. Paul, incidentally, had some rather unkind words about the Christians at Corinth who anticipated the festivities of the Eucharist with a little too much of what the Irish call "creature."

The pentecostals and the cursillos are a reaction against the dull, dry neurotic spirituality of the past. When reason tries to rule as a tyrant, it is bound to have a revolution. But now the tyrant is overthrown, and emotionality runs amuck without any restraining force.

Similarly, group dynamics hold immense potential for growth and trust and openness, but the survey research on sensitivity training indicates that at best it has only moderate influence, and then, generally only on strong and well-integrated personalities. When practiced by amateurs working with shallow, confused, or disoriented personalities, it can do immense harm.

The clergy and the religious have been isolated from the human condition and taught to repress their emotions for too long. Yet the clerical teeny-bopper or Don Juan and the religious flirt are no more authentic human beings than were their desiccated predecessors.

Authority, if it is to be effective, cannot, as Father McKenzie has recently pointed out, disassociate itself from the human condition. Structures in any organization must be flexible and open to growth. Moral principles have to be applied to concrete realities, and the theology that is not "actual," as Cardinal Danielou said some twenty years ago, is no theology at all.

Nevertheless, human society cannot survive without leadership, without established patterns of behavior, without ethical norms, and without theoretical statements of values and goals. Leadership, structure, ethics, theoretical values, are difficult to articulate, and even more difficult to reformulate in times of change. The anti-intellectual romanticist is impatient; he does not have the time—nor, if the truth be told, the personality structure—to work at the hard task of growth and change. Everything must be changed at once, and if it doesn't change at once, well, then, there's only one solution left: blow your mind, man!

Roman Catholicism in the United States, then, is engaged in a colossal revolt against reason, a revolt that is particularly strong among the clergy and the religious and the younger laity, but seems to be permeating all levels of the Church—left and right, young and old, rich and poor, powerful and weak. Not everybody has blown his mind, of course, but the irrationalists seem to be in the ascendancy, and he who attempts to reason with them finds himself at a distinct disadvantage.

For rationality has already been ruled out of court—along with civility, docility, fidelity, and other square virtues. By the very fact that you attempt to engage in rational discourse with the romanticists, you have proven yourself a square, and squares are not to be taken seriously. The only way you can know about things is if you make a cursillo or go to a pentecostal meeting or engage in sensitivity training or smoke pot or find yourself a girl friend or mistress, or at least engage in a little bit of casual philandering. You gotta tune in, man, turn on, man; you gotta tell it like it is; you gotta see things the way they are; you gotta feel; you gotta have heart; you gotta be open and honest and trustworthy, and above all, sincere. You've got to *care*. As for thinking—why, man, that's square stuff.

But if it is impossible to engage in rational dialogue with the irrationalists—impossible almost by very definition—it is still necessary for those of us who believe in human reason to attempt to understand what the roots of the new irrationality are. Romanticism is, of course, very much a part of the spirit of the times; the fascist storm troopers of the SDS are hailed as radicals and progressives. Eldridge Cleaver, a self-confessed rapist, is awarded the accolade of prophet. Hatred, as long as it comes from blacks, is to be applauded. All police are pigs, and the collective orgy at Woodstock, New York, is the sign of an emerging positive "counter culture." When such ideas are enthusiastically accepted in the larger American society, it is small wonder that within the Catholic community we produce our own little brand of second-rate romanticism.

But there are some twists to it that are uniquely our own. Catholicism is burdened with a substantial number of clergy and religious whose emotional maturation was aborted in their late teens by the seminary and novitiate experience. The fixation of their emotions in late adolescence was not a complete disaster as long as the rigidly structured Church sustained their personalities. But many of the rigid structures have been swept away by the Vatican Council's renewal program, with the result that the Church suddenly finds itself with a considerable number of professional personnel who are, psychologically speaking, still very much adolescent. It is not dysfunctional to be psychologically adolescent when you are chronologically adolescent, but to be psychologically adolescent when you are chronologically adult can be intolerable. Many of our adolescent clergy and religious cannot tolerate complexity or ambiguity. They seek simple solutions, magic answers, instant competence, and overnight maturity. There is little in the way of firm inner core to their personality, and not much in the way of convictions or commitments to shore them up. The romanticism that is surging across the country is just what they're looking for.

The Catholic intelligentsia—that is to say, those who deal in some fashion or other with ideas—have not protested very vigorously against the blowing-your-mind syndrome. Indeed, a large segment of the American intelligentsia has refused to resist the romanticist fads and fashions. Catholic intellectuals are too busy blaming the hierarchy, engaging in shrill and strident criticism, and making folk heroes out of defecting clergymen to realize that, in the final analysis, the anti-rationalism of the time will erode the precarious base of reason on which they, like all intellectuals, stand.

Finally, ecclesiastical leadership is too busy wringing its hands, closing issues, condemning abuses, and forbidding changes to realize that it has really lost not only control, but credibility. If the leadership had been able to read the "signs of the times" and respond to them, then the romantic heretics would not have been able to seize center stage. But the leadership was not aware—or did not choose to be aware—of the implications of the hunger for relevance, meaning, community, relationship, integrity, dialogue, authenticity, and all the other ideas that are so important in the modern world.

Leadership did not interpret the signs of the times. It did not respond to the presence of the Spirit. It did not search out the charisma.
And so the heretics took charge and converted the signs of the times
into slogans and clichés—and in the process, threw rationality, sen-
sibility, and civility out the window.

The mind blowing that is so characteristic of American Catholicism at the start of the seventies, is merely evidence of a desperate
search for meaning among people who lack convictions, and a desperate search for community among people who lack a sense of
personal integrity. They seek experience to validate their reality and
other people's affection in order to validate their goodness. James
Kavanaugh, so pathetically desperate to find a wife so that he could
prove himself a man, surely was not a man for all seasons, but alas, it
is very much feared that he may be a man for our season. He may have
been the first of the Catholic romantics, the first to blow his mind,
but he surely will not be the last.

David Riesman, one of the few American intellectuals who has
vigorously resisted the irrationalism of our present romantic era, has
recently remarked that it would be a shame if the rationality of the
Jesuit colleges was completely replaced by sensitivity training; he has
also lamented the irrationality displayed by many young priests and
religious. There is in Riesman's comments something rather nostalgic,
for he can remember, as does any educated man, the fact that the
Catholic Church for a millennium or more defended the validity
of human reason against the assault of barbarians. The new barbarians, however, seem to be as much inside the Church as outside it.
Catholicism has always insisted that man was rational, that he was
specifically distinguished from the other animals by his rationality.
There is no denying that in more recent times Catholic insistence
on rationality has been converted to insistence on canonical juridicism. Nor is there any denying that Catholicism seemed for a
while to lose its awareness of the powers of the Spirit and of the
importance of human emotions; that Church which for a thousand
years or more defended not only rationality, but also, and simultaneously, the liturgical and mystical traditions, lost at the end of its

post-Byzantine era a vital linkage with science, with the sacred, with the mystical, and with the human body (which body it had vigorously defended against the Manichaeans and the Jansenists). It is unable to defend human reason now, as it did in the past, because it, too, committed the crime of the modern world; it permitted reason to be divorced from feeling, from spirit, and from the sacred. Whether our liturgical, mystical, and scholarly traditions are strong enough in the United States at the present time to turn back the irrationalities of the barbarians, remains to be seen. It is much more likely that we are going to have to let mind blowing run its course.

In other words, we blew it.

2.   A New Chance for the Sacred?

During a recent unpleasantness between the University of Chicago and its SDS, the normal, decorous quiet of the Social Science building was rent one fine afternoon by ear-piercing shrieks. Secretaries, research assistants, and even a few faculty members dashed to their office doors to discover who was being murdered. Three young women dressed in shabby and tattered garments were standing in front of the Sociology Department office shrieking curses: "Fie on thee, Morris Janowitz! A hex on thy strategy!"

WITCH (Women's International Terrorist Conspiracy from Hell) had come to put a curse on the Sociology Department.

So far, nothing seems to have happened to Professor Janowitz or the Sociology Department. But if it does, there are going to be an awful lot of frightened people along the Midway. (I offered as a matter of professional courtesy to sprinkle holy water on the departmental office, but, while social science is ready for witchcraft, it is not yet ready for exorcism.)

WITCH is but one manifestation—though a spectacular one—of a resurgence of interest in the occult on the college campuses of the country. Although some observers of WITCH's "hexing" dismiss them as a form of "guerrilla theater," the Witches themselves attempt to be more serious. They elaborate a quasi-scholarly explanation of how they continue a neolithic religion that worshipped the great earth mother goddess until it was replaced by Christianity. One suspects that the Witches are but first cousins of the California Druids, who also claim to be carrying on a tradition from the neolithic underground—thus confounding those of us who thought that the only Druids left in the world were Irish monsignors.

WITCH may be a put-on. One has the impression that its members are not even sure themselves how seriously they take their witchcraft. Like most of the other manifestations of the neosacred around the country, WITCH is a combination of the put-on and the serious, of the deliberately comic and the profoundly agonized, of the bizarre and the holy.

Item. Professor Huston Smith of Massachusetts Institute of Technology in his chapter "Secularization and the Sacred" from *The Religious Situation* (edited by Donald R. Cutler, Beacon Press, 1968) describes an experience with a seminar of some of the best students in the institution.

. . . I cannot recall the exact progression of topics, but it went something like this: Beginning with Asian philosophy, it moved on to meditation, then yoga, then Zen, then Tibet, then successively to the *Bardo Thodol*, tantra, the kundalini, the chakras, the *I Ching*, karate and aikido, the yang-yin, macrobiotic (brown rice) diet, Gurdjieff, Meher Baba, astrology, astral bodies, auras, UFO's, tarot cards, parapsychology, witchcraft, and magic. And, underlying everything, of course, the psychedelic drugs. Nor were the students dallying with these subjects. They were *on* the drugs; they were eating brown rice; they were meditating hours on end; they were making their decisions by *I Ching* divination, which one student designated the most important discovery of his life; they were constructing complicated electronic experiments to prove that their thoughts, via psychokinesis, could affect matter directly.

And they weren't plebeians. Intellectually they were aristocrats, with the highest average math scores in the land, Ivy League verbal scores, and two to three years of saturation in MIT science.

Item. A certain Catholic university discovered that it had a coven of warlocks on campus (warlocks, for the uninitiated, are male witches). As the dean of the institution put it, "We've really become progressive around here. A couple of hundred years ago we would have burned them at the stake. Twenty-five years ago I would have expelled them. Now we simply sent them all to psychiatrists."

Item. At a Canadian university, the student body was given a chance to recommend courses of its own choosing to be included in the curriculum. The majority of the courses had to do with the sacred—astrology, Zen, sorcery, and witchcraft.

Item. In most of the elite universities in the country, horoscopes and the prediction of the future by the use of tarot cards are widespread. Not all the students, not even a majority, are engaging in such divination. But a minority are, and the majority do not ridicule their efforts. On the contrary, one has the impression that the majority react the same way they react to the SDS: "We understand why they want to do it, even if we are not yet ready to do it ourselves."

Item. Catholic girls' colleges seem to be particularly disposed to producing groups of young women who make decisions by use of the ancient Chinese method of the *I Ching*.[1]

Item. In a number of colleges, particularly in California, semi-monastic cults have arisen composed of young people who subsist on vegetarian diets, take vows not to cut their hair, and spend long hours in contemplation.

Item. A thin network of students have formed a loose "community" to support one another through the ardors of graduate school, a community that does not take spatial separation to be a very serious problem in the providing of mutual support. One leader of the "community" describes quite bluntly what the "community" is about: "You might say we're forming a new religious order."

[1] In class, I mistakenly pronounced it "eye" but a student gently rebuked me after class and informed me that it would be pronounced "eee." The *I Ching*, by the way, is an ancient Chinese divination device that enables one to make decisions—a sort of pre-IBM computer.

Item. In the hills of Sonoma, there flourishes an institution called the "Six Day School," composed largely of Berkeley dropouts, who learn about political pacifism, astrology, vegetarian dieting, mysticism, and magic, during the course of their stay at the school—which usually exceeds six days. One group last year left Sonoma to proceed to Mount Shasta, there to await the end of the world. They may not have worn white robes, but the repeated predictions of the end of the world or at least the end of California lead one to believe that in the Golden State it may not have been 1969, but rather 999.[2]

I remarked in one of my classes that I had been able to locate almost every kind of off-beat religious behavior on our campus save for spiritualistic séances, and wondered why, especially after Bishop Pike's book, someone hadn't thought of hunting up a medium. Several members of the class promptly assured their confreres that I hadn't looked very far; spiritualism was alive and well in Hyde Park.

What (you should excuse the expression) the hell is going on?

Perhaps the most puzzling aspect of the new pursuit of the sacred is that it is so funny and yet so serious. Students cannot talk about it without laughing, and yet they must interrupt their laughter to protest that they respect the goals of the new devotees of the sacred. However, the puzzle is less difficult when one understands that the cultists are engaging in a form of *drama*—partly, one suspects, under the influence of their cousins, the hippies. Drama about the sacred is *liturgy*; and liturgy, as J. Huizinga pointed out in his famous book *Homo Ludens*, is sacred play. The sacred by its very nature has large components of the playful and the comic close to its core. Only with the Reformation did the idea that the sacred was grimly serious finally triumph in the Western world. Catholic clerics will probably

[2] It was generally believed that the world would come to an end on January 1 in the year 1000. Unfortunately for those who had expected that the world would only survive one millennium of Christianity, the monk who had set up the Julian calendar was five years off his calculations. But the world didn't end in either 995 or 1000. Historians say that, curiously enough, about the only place in Europe that did not shut down on December 31, 999, was the Vatican.

admit, now that the venerable Solemn High Mass has fallen into disuse, that they frequently found it hard to keep a straight face during its complex ceremonies. The new manifestations of the sacred, like the Solemn High Mass, are simultaneously much in earnest and a hilarious put-on. To put a hex on the Sociology Department is comic, but it is also a tentative assertion that there are powers in Heaven and on Earth that may transcend sociology departments.

Let us, first of all, make all the proper qualifications. Only a minority of students are engaged in the pursuit of the bizarrely sacred. Such pursuit is not new among young people, but is a continuation of the interest in the occult and the mystical that has persisted for some time. It is a form of romanticism that has recurred in one fashion or another periodically in years gone by. It is experimental, and does not indicate any return to the organized churches; as one student said to me, "Who in the world would expect to find anything sacred in the churches?"

The evidence for this resurgence of interest in the sacred is "impressionistic" and not yet based on the kind of "hard" empirical data that so delight the heart of the social scientist. Nevertheless, with all these qualifications, it still does seem that there has been a very notable increase, however temporary, in interest in the sacred, and particularly the bizarrely sacred, among students on the college and university campuses in the past few years. Furthermore, the "return of the sacred" has happened exactly where one would least expect it: among the elite students at the best colleges and universities in the land—precisely those places where secularization would presumably have been most effective and most complete.

One repeats the question: What the hell is going on? God is dead, but the devil lives?

One of the things that strikes an interviewer who talks to students about the "return of the sacred" is their firm insistence on taking it seriously, even though they may themselves not be involved in witchcraft, astrology, or the *I Ching*. They resolutely refuse to dismiss those who are as foolish. On the contrary, the sacred, like just about everything else, must be taken very seriously in student bull sessions.

The first reason that young people give for the "return of the sacred" is the failure of science. One graduate student said to me, "Let's face it, science is dead. While the newspapers and magazines were giving all the attention to the death of God, science was really the one that was dying."

The extent and the depth of the revolts against positivism come as a considerable shock to those, such as I, whose training in the positive sciences took place in a time when they were totally unquestioned at the great universities. During the winter quarter, I put a statistical table on the blackboard and proceeded to explain the implications. One of my students respectfully but pointedly observed, "Mr.[3] Greeley, I think you're an empiricist. In fact, at times I even think you are a *naive* empiricist." The accusation didn't surprise me, because I guess I am an empiricist, but the tone of it did, for it was a tone of voice that used to reserved for the accusation of being a "clerical fascist."

The student then went on to deliver a fierce harangue against "the epistemology of science," and to assert that the "imperialism" of science, by which it claimed to be the only valid form of human knowledge and the only valid rationale for organizing society, was completely unsatisfactory to his generation. A number of other students rose to offer vigorous support to this position.

After class I pondered the matter in some confusion, and returned the following session to ask if there was anyone who disagreed. Would no one rise with the appropriate quote from Casper Nagel to defend empiricism, positivism, and rationality? The class was completely silent, until one young woman remarked, "I think we all agree with what was said in the last class." At the beginning of the 1960s, when I was in graduate school, such thoughts would have been "thinking the unthinkable."

The young people seem to be angry at science for its failures. A

---

[3] The appropriate title for a University of Chicago faculty member—whatever his sacred or canonical status.

coed observed, "Science hasn't ended war, it hasn't ended injustice, and it doesn't respond to most of man's needs. Why should we take it seriously?" And another joined in: "Pure rationalism just isn't rational, because man is more than reason, and religion knows that, even if positive science doesn't." And yet a third coed concluded, "Science was something that we had to work through our system. It only started with people like Darwin, and it's not surprising that for a while everybody thought it was the only thing that mattered. It's just now that we've come to know better."

One may disagree with such an indictment of science, and yet when Berger, the hero of *Hair*, says, "Screw your science, screw your rationality," he speaks for many of his generation.

Some other students explained the return to the sacred as a reaction to the failure of the university administrations and faculty to live up to their own rationalist and scientific principles. A young man put it this way: "When we see the utter incapacity of the rationalists to engage in rational discourse with us, we begin to rediscover the legitimacy of emotions. From that is just a short step to the legitimacy of the sacred."

The rhetoric of the return to the sacred is not so very different from the rhetoric of the radical political movements. Words such as "honesty," "integrity," "fidelity," "love," "openness," and "community" abound. The hippie culture, with its emphasis on drugs, stands midway between the two, bridging the gap between and pervading both other movements with its influence. Yet the movements are distinct. The hippies and the radicals may frequently use religious terminology and even respond to "religious needs," but their concerns still tend to be this-worldly. The neosacralists, on the other hand, are willing to accept as a working possibility a world that, if it does not completely transcend the present world, at least to some extent stands beyond it.

It is precisely this "standing beyond" that young people relate to the second reason for the return to the sacred: The sacred seems to provide an avenue for personal efficacy. As a male undergraduate described it, "Why use the *I Ching* in a world where you have the IBM 360? The answer is easy. You can't understand the 360 and you don't have much control over it. The *I Ching* says that there are powers that stand beyond and are more powerful than the 360, powers with which in some way you can enter into a meaningful relationship when you can't do it with the 360." And one of his friends added, "Most of us realize that other people make our decisions for us quite arbitrarily. Whether I go to Vietnam or not, whether I get killed there or not, doesn't depend at all on who I am or what I think. I'd sooner feel that my future was being shaped by the stars or by the turn of the cards, because these would represent powers that would be more concerned about me than would either my draft board or the Pentagon."

I pressed these two young men to question whether they really did think that there was something beyond that made itself known through the movements of the stars or the turn of the cards. One of them shrugged uncomfortably. "I'm not sure," he said, "but I like to think so." And the other commented, "It's like the conclusion of Arthur Miller's *Death of a Salesman.* In death, somebody did 'notice' Willy Loman. When someone turns the cards for you, you feel at least here you are being noticed."

The theme that religion is a response to alienation and to a feeling of unimportance in the larger society is widespread in the students' comments. "Religion makes you feel like you're a *person*," a woman undergraduate told me. "It makes you feel that you are important and that what you do does matter and you can have influence on others." Students are further impressed by the enthusiasm and confidence of the cultists. "They really believe that what they say is *true*," observed one young man to me. "They really believe that they do have the answer and that they do know what is ethically right and ethically wrong. It's hard to avoid being affected by their enthusiasm after you've been in a school that really isn't sure what is true or what is right or wrong."

Like the radicals and the hippies, the neosacralists are in desperate search for something to belong to. The religious groups are *communities*, places where you are more than just an IBM file card. A young woman put it this way: "If you get into a group like that, you at least know that somebody will notice the difference if you're murdered. Around this university, you could be dead in your room for days and nobody would ever know the difference." And another commented, "We don't have to worry any more, at least not very much, about where our food and housing is going to come from, so we worry about ourselves and about finding ourselves. The only place where we are going to find ourselves is in deep relationships with others, and that means either religion or sex and maybe both." The religious communities that grew up around the various cults of the sacred are felt to provide opportunities for meaningful intimate relationships, over against the depersonalizing formalism of the academic and governmental bureaucracies. "You're a *person* in the group even if you don't want to be. You're forced to face yourself and discover who you are."

The quest for community in small groups makes the neosacralists quite conscious of the relevance to their quest of T-groups, encounter groups, and the whole bag of group-dynamics tricks. Just as for some students group dynamics or sensitive training becomes almost a religion, so for others already involved in quasi-religious behavior, sensitivity training and its cousins become an important means of religious growth. One girl told me how delighted she was to be part of a T-group that included two people who were on drugs and two others who were making their major decisions by means of horoscopes. It was, she noted, a fascinating experience. One does not doubt it in the least.

Underlying the other three explanations the young people offer for the return to the sacred is a fourth: The sacred provides meaning. "In one way," a charming young woman said to me, "the sacred is even better than drugs, because when you're on drugs the world looks beautiful to you only if you're on a trip and ugly when you're not on a trip. But religion has persuaded some people that the world is beautiful most of the time, despite the ugliness we see. That's terribly important." And one of her male classmates chimed in, "What we're really concerned about is whether anything is real; I mean, whether it is *really real*. Is there something that is so powerful that it can even make *us* real?" And an older graduate student (a clergyman, I suspect, but nowadays it's hard to tell) pointed out, "And Mircea Eliade [Professor of History of Religions at the University of Chicago and one of the world's most distinguished experts on the sacred] tells us that this is exactly what the sacred is, the *really* real."

Some of those who have kept an eye on WITCH argue that its principal contribution is to give its members some sense of what it means to be a woman, even if it is a bizarre concept of womanhood. Full meaning not only involves understanding what the world is all about or at least understanding whether the world has anything in it that is "really real," but also involves having some sense of what you are all about and whether there is a possibility that you are "really real." The religious experience, in the final analysis, is seen as "ecstatic," that is to say, that it, like sex, takes a person out of himself and brings him into contact not only with other human beings but with the "creative powers" that presumably underpin the cosmos.

My very unsystematic survey of student opinion on the neosacred leads me to conclude that what is going on is authentically, if perhaps transiently and bizarrely, religious. Personal efficacy, meaning, community, encounter with the ecstatic and the transcendental, and the refusal to believe that mere reason can explain either life or personhood—all of these have traditionally been considered religious postures. An anthropologist from another planet visiting the secular university campus could not help but conclude that there was a lot of very interesting religious behavior going on, and, like Professor Smith, he would probably feel that it was very primal and primordial, if not indeed primitive, religious behavior. Do they believe in God? I have the impression that most of the young neosacralists would not understand the question or at least would find it premature. They

don't believe in the God they left behind in their parish congregations. But they are frankly experimenting—as a part of a self-
conscious "psychosocial moratorium"—with the "experience of the
sacred" to see whether there is anything there that could add depth
and richness to their lives. Most of them seem to hope, at times
rather forlornly, that they will be able to find something or Something. But they are not ready to give it or It a name just yet.

The new religious enthusiasts clearly owe a major debt of gratitude to the hippies. Indeed, one might even consider them to be
merely one wing of the hippie movement. Both emphasize the prerational, if not the anti-rational. The quest for the spontaneous and
the "natural" in the two dissenting groups is a protest against the
"hang-ups" of a society that is viewed as overorganized and over-
rationalized, but less than human. Both are a search for "experience,"
and for a specific kind of experience—one that "takes one out of oneself." Both have, as we noted before, a strong comic element about
them—an irresistible urge to "put on" the rational society.

Both the neosacralists and the hippies are communitarian, seeking experience and vitality from intimate friendships, friendships that
in many instances are strongly at odds with the conventions of the
larger society. The two groups are further linked by their longing for
the mystical and the reflective, again because these activities are seen
as a means of standing apart from the rest of society, which has so
little time for anything else but activity. The ceremonies, the rituals,
even the *vestments* of the two groups also represent a common
revolt against the sober and somber garb of the suburban business-
man and his daily schedule. (Long hair used to be important, but
now that even the suburban executive is wearing sideburns and
maybe a goatee, we might expect the deviants to imitate Buddhist
monks and shave their heads.)

So the new search for the sacred shares with the hippies an "acted-
out" rejection of the rationalized bourgeois society, a rejection that
is also a put-on of that society. The hippies were the first to become
concerned with the mystical and the occult. But many of the new
religious enthusiasts are not hippies in the ordinary sense of the

word, and most of them are not willing to go the "drug route" with the hippies. Some say quite frankly that they view religion as a substitute for drugs, and one that is much less dangerous. One hesitates to say it, but the neosacralists appear to be much more "respectable" than the hippies.

But the important difference, I think, is that the religious cultists are seeking for something that hippies refuse to be hung up on; they seem to be looking for what the sociologists would call a "meaning system" or an "interpretative scheme." The hippies put on life because they think life is a put-on and ought not to be taken seriously. Those who are engaging in the quest for the sacred are, with a greater or lesser amount of explicit acknowledgment of the fact, looking for an explanation for life and for themselves. They're not sure they'll find it; they're not even sure that the search is anything more than a joke. But they'd like to think it just might be.

Two groups have been caught off base by the resurgence of the sacred: the campus clergy, be they ministers, priests, or divinity students, and the Roman Catholic Church. The former, having bought lock, stock, and barrel the idea that science and secularization had eliminated the sacred from the human condition, have been vigorously pursuing "relevance" with militant radical politics. They now discover, much to their surprise, that a fair number of young people are looking for gurus—holy men. As one black-haired coed observed only half facetiously, "You really don't expect a divinity-school student or a seminarian to be a holy man, but you've got to give them credit for it. Some of them are at least beginning to try once again."

But the Roman Catholic Church has really been caught flat-footed. Its so-called intellectual avant-garde, taking Harvey Cox far more seriously than he ever took himself, have been busy dismantling all traces of the sacred and the mystical in their "underground" religious communities. Thus the Roman Church, the master for more than a millennium of a great tradition of liturgy and mysticism, finds itself putting off vestments just when the rest of the world is putting them on, abandoning ceremony just as the neosacralists are beginning to form their own ceremonies, and downgrading the sacred precisely at the time that some students at the elite universities are rediscovering it. Furthermore, it is very doubtful that an authentic mystic could possibly be ordained a priest of the Roman Catholic Church in the United States at the present time. He would certainly be failed out of the seminary because of his inability to adjust to his T-group. Greeley's First Law seems to apply perfectly to the relationship between American Catholicism and the sacred: "American Catholics stop something just at a time other people are starting it."[4] But after one has lamented the sad plight of the enthusiastic secularists within the organized churches, one is still forced to face the issue of why the search for community, efficacy, meaning, and experience took a religious turn, particularly in an environment in which one would have least expected it. Why did the sacred rise up once again precisely at the time when it seemed to be just about in its last agony?

It might be more pertinent to ask why we are so surprised about the return of the sacred. The non-rational has been with man a long time, and so have the supernatural and even the superstitious. Was it not unduly naive of us to assume that it would disappear so quickly? Astrology has always been a rather successful industry. Superstition is widespread in the general population. More than two fifths of the American population go to church every week, as do almost half the college students in the country. The limited amount of longitudinal research done on religious beliefs and behavior shows very little change in the past two decades. If the sacred and the superstitious still permeate the larger society, why are we so surprised that they have been tenacious enough to reassert themselves on the college campus?

Students themselves will cheerfully admit that their lives are not at all free from superstitious behavior, even if they don't take the sacred or the supernatural very seriously. As one girl said to me, "I

---

[4] Greeley's Second Law is also relevant: "American Catholics start something just when other people are about to stop it."

always wear the same sweatshirt every time I take an exam, and I know other people who simply refuse to go into an exam unless they've had a shower beforehand. When you ask us why we do these things, the only response we can come up with is, Why not? Sure it might not make any difference, but then again it might, and there's no point in taking any chances." One is reminded of the famous agnostic prayer addressed "To whom it may concern."

My friend Peter H. Rossi, Chairman of the Sociology Department at Johns Hopkins University, summarized only half facetiously the relationship between agnosticism and superstition: "I'm not sure that I believe in good spirits, but I have the uncanny feeling that there might be evil spirits."

Journalists, ministry students, theologians, and senior faculty members may have been far too hasty in buying a simple-minded evolutionary version of "growth" from the sacred to the secular. As Seymour Martin Lipset points out in his famous essay on American religion, the sacred and the profane have been able to co-exist more or less harmoniously in American religion for most of the nation's existence. And Professor Clifford Geertz expressed the anthropologist's suspicion of how new agnosticism really is when he suggested that a book ought to be written someday about belief and unbelief in primitive societies that would have as a subtitle "Faith and Hypocrisy Among Primitive Men."

Similarly, Talcott Parsons argues persuasively that the so-called secularization process does not represent in fact a decline in the importance of religion, but merely a "differentiation," in which religion assumes those functions that are specific to it—the providing of meaning and belonging—where other functions that it had in the past are assumed by newer corporate institutions. Edward Shils of the University of Chicago summarizes the argument for the persistence of the sacred:

> I venture the opinion that, in a variety of ways, it will survive. As long as the category of the "serious" remains in human life, there will be a profound impulse to acknowledge and express an appreciation

of the "seriousness" which puts the individual into contact with words and actions of symbolic import.

It is this sense of the "serious" which constitutes the religious impulse in man. This I regard as given in the constitution of man in the same way that cognitive powers are given or locomotive powers are given. (Edward Shils, "Ritual and Crisis," in *The Religious Situation*, Boston, 1968, p. 747.)

Similarly, Huston Smith, attempting to analyze his experience with the polymorphously religious seminar at MIT, thinks that the strain toward the sacred is persistent in the human condition:

What I learned was that the human mind stands ready to believe anything—absolutely anything—as long as it provides an alternative to the totally desacralized mechanomorphic outlook of objective science. Some may see the lesson as teaching no more than the extent of human credulity. I read it otherwise. If mechanomorphism is the truth, then indeed the students' behavior reveals no more than man's unwillingness to accept it. But if being *is* sacred, or potentially sacred, the students' phrenetic thrusts suggest something different. In things of the spirit, subject and object mesh exceptionally. No faith, no God; without response, revelation doesn't exist. It follows that the sacred depends, not entirely but in part, on man's nose for it. Given noses as keen for the chase as were those students', if the sacred lurks anywhere in the marshes of contemporary life, it is going to be flushed out. Or better—because it goes further in bridging the subject-object dichotomy—drives which are this strong help to *generate* the sacred.

It may be, therefore, that our surprise about the survival of the sacred, indeed its apparent rebirth at the secular campus, is based on a very naive model of man. Reason cannot rule the human personality as a tyrant. It must either govern the emotions, either mystical or orgiastic, as a constitutional monarch, or it will run the risk of being overthrown in a revolution. The non-rational on the campus, be it drugs, political violence, or tarot cards, is evidence that man has not evolved beyond the sacred and may not yet, at least for a little while—or perhaps ever.

Not everyone needs or wants the sacred, certainly not at the present time, and probably not in the past either. In Shils's words:

> . . . they [the powers of the religious impulse] are unevenly given and unevenly cultivated, so that the sense of the "serious," the need for contact with the charismatic or sacred values, differs markedly among human beings within any society. Some persons, a minority, tend to have it to a pronounced degree and even relatively continuously; others, far more numerous, will experience it only intermittently and, except rarely, without great intensity. Finally there is a minority which is utterly opaque to the serious. . . . They have already shown much greater tenacity than nineteenth-century positivists and utilitarians assumed. The need for order, and for meaning in order, are too fundamental in man for the human race as a whole to allow itself to be bereft of the rich and elaborate scheme of metaphorical interpretation of existence which is made available by the great world religions. The spread of education and of scientific knowledge, as well as the improved level of material well-being, will not eradicate them unless those who have these religions in their charge lose their self-confidence because of the distrust the highly educated hold toward the inherited metaphors.

The critical question, then, might very well be not why has the return to the sacred happened, but can the positivistic, rationalistic society, and particularly its academic and religious institutions, assimilate and understand what the resurrection of the sacred seems to mean: Not by reason alone doth man live.

Will the interest in the sacred on the college campus survive? For some individual students, it is clearly nothing more than an experiment that is part of their youthful "psychosocial moratorium," a part of their quest for personal identity. If the data on graduate-student church attendance are to be believed, the moratorium will end not so much with agnosticism or even a new form of religion for most students, but rather a return to some form of traditional religion. (A recent NORC survey of graduate students showed that about 40 per cent of the students at the twelve major arts and science graduate schools in the country were regular church attenders.) Witchcraft, astrology, and divination, if they lose at all, are likely to lose to the traditional religions, in spite of scientific secularism.[5]

Yet, some of the present concern about the sacred is likely to continue influencing the traditional church system within—perhaps even lead to the formation of new religious sects. Like almost everything else on campus, the return to the sacred, while it is communitarian, is profoundly anti-organizational. Whatever of the present commitment to the sacred survives, is likely to be informal and casual, but such groups as the Druids and WITCH could conceivably grow much larger.

The students, in any event, have little doubt that the sacred will continue to interest them and that it will continue to fascinate their successors on campus. As one undergraduate male argued, "The interest in the sacred is rooted in a kind of existentialist dissatisfaction with the way things are, and since the way things are is not likely to change for a while, there is no reason to think the sacred is going to go away either." Certainly the dissatisfaction with the failures of positive science does not seem to be reversible, and one is inclined to suspect that it will be a fairly long time before the argument that religion or the supernatural or the sacred is not "scientific" will be persuasive. Not everybody will be religious, but neither will religion be in full retreat; and some of the more bizarre, primitive, and superstitious forms of the religious are likely to enjoy a certain respectability for a number of years to come.

Most of the contemporary manifestations of the sacred on the college and university campus are a form of withdrawal from the larger society—if not positively destructive in their view of said society. Yet the constructivist element is not completely absent. I remarked a few weeks ago to my seminar on the sociology of religion

[5] The NORC data also showed that physical scientists and biological scientists are more likely to be religious than those in the humanities and the social sciences, suggesting that the battle between science and religion may be more severe in the "soft" sciences than in the "hard" ones.

that I thought most of the new religious forms offered personal redemption but despaired of social redemption. One young woman raised her hand. "Mr. Greeley," she asked, "have you ever heard of a book called *The Phenomenon of Man*, by a man named Teilhard de Chardin?" I admitted that I had. "Well," she said, "I was deeply impressed by that book because even though there is so much wrong with the world right now, I think Teilhard is right when he says that we're on the verge of a great leap into a much better form of human life, that we are moving into the noosphere and that we are traveling toward an omega point. I think there's a lot of us that feel that we can have a faith in the sacred which will help us to create a better world."

I admitted to being something of a Teilhardist myself and conceded that there might be some of what she described in the student quest for the sacred, but insisted that I didn't see much of it and that I felt the "return of the sacred" assumed largely that the world was unredeemable and discriminating.

That was a mistake, for all kinds of hands rose up in the seminar room, and all kinds of students rose up to assert their faith in the possibility of a Teilhard-like vision of evolution toward the omega point.

I still can't quite figure out the meaning of that experience, but I must say I never expected to encounter a classroom of Teilhardists at the University of Chicago. Such people are necessarily a minority—a very small minority—of the whole student population, or indeed of the whole population of the world. There are not very many Teilhardists around. But it wouldn't take very many . . .

It might just turn out to be the age of Aquarius after all. . . .

3. The Bread of Faith

Dietrich Bonhoeffer's notion of "religionless man" is one of the more quaint myths of our era. Religionless man is not merely man without faith but man who does not need an Ultimate, and who does not even need to ask ultimate questions. He is secular man, master of all he surveys, privy to the secrets of the universe, governed by rationality, pushing back the frontiers of knowledge by the scientific method, subsisting in a world that needs no explanation beyond itself. He controls the rivers and the seas, dominates the earth, reduces all its life to his service, lands on the moon, and is about to bring even the weather under his control. As an ultimate tribute to his brilliance, he has devised computers that, it is claimed, are even more brilliant than he is.[1]

[1] One of the untold tragedies of modern times is the number of small and medium-sized businesses that have been seriously harmed, if not destroyed, by computerization. The recent failure of a number of major Wall Street houses is in part because the computers did not live up to the promises of the computer salesmen. It is but the tip of the iceberg. Computers are fine when they work, but as someone who has been plagued with them for a decade and never had a smoothly functioning computer system available, I am prepared to assert that computers are a myth. The classic example of the value of the computer is the first moon landing, when, in the last thirty seconds, the damned computer on the machine broke down and told the astronauts to abort the landing, a command that fortunately was rejected by the common sense of the human pilots.

As a matter of fact, one could almost say the classic picture of religionless man is the computer programmer poring over his "print-outs" as the killer smog begins to close in on his cubicle; but, at least before the smog gets to him, religionless man doesn't need myth, doesn't need transcendence, doesn't need the sacred. Indeed, it is not so much that he has considered these possibilities and rejected them; they are, rather, possibilities that he deems not even worth considering.

To complement the myth of religionless man, we have the myth of mythological man, who, it is presumed, went out of business some time before 1950. Not only did mythological man believe; he believed almost everything. He saw angels and demons around every bend, and behind every bush. He was a superstitious ignoramus who had little scientific knowledge and less ability to manipulate his environment. His belief in myths and the transcendent and the sacred was rooted in his fear of the unknown and his inability to bring the environment under control. While not exactly subhuman, he surely was not as fully human as modern religionless man. He was, at best, unenlightened.

All this, of course, is a little hard on the artistic geniuses who created the cave paintings of Lascaux by candlelight, and the scientific geniuses who created the great observatory at Stonehenge, but Stonehenge was a temple, and so probably was Lascaux, so obviously these men were unenlightened.

Religionless man is currently in trouble, however. Empirical research has not been able to discover very many of the sociological theories of authors such as Edward Shils, Clifford Geertz, Peter Berger, and Thomas Luckman, who would suggest that religionless man is, at best, likely to be a very small minority of the human race for the foreseeable future. Langdon Gilkey, in his brilliant *Naming the Whirlwind*, demonstrates quite conclusively that in the very concept of secularity there is a demand for an ultimate explanation. In Gilkey's words:

> Both these secular alternatives of optimism and despair are, however, untrue to the experienced texture of our existence. Life seems

in a baffling and mysterious way to share both creativity and sin, wonder and terror, joy and despair and, in the midst of its fateful tragedy, to reveal facets of hope, renewal and love. This strange characteristic of life, secularism seems not to comprehend—with its alternating optimism about man's rational and moral powers as a maker of history and its despair at our loneliness in a cold, ruthless world. We are neither so good and so powerful as the optimistic secularist says, nor is life so empty and futile as the pessimistic secularist declares, and the problem with both answers is that they have cut man off from his roots, they have tried to understand him on his own terms alone, without the dimension of ultimacy, sacrality which makes a man, and so, without comprehending either the creative resources or the demonic distortions which that dimension provides to his life. (Langdon Gilkey, *Naming the Whirlwind*. Indianapolis: Bobbs-Merrill, 1969, p. 259.)

And if modern man turns out to be not quite so religionless after all, neither was pre-1950 man all that unhesitatingly credulous. Joseph Ratzinger, in his *Introduction to Christianity*, speaks of Teresa of Lisieux:

. . . who looks so naive and unproblematical, had grown up in an atmosphere of complete religious security; her whole existence from beginning to end, and down to the smallest details, was so completely moulded by the faith of the Church that the invisible world had become not just a part of her everyday life, but that life itself. . . . Yet this very saint, a person apparently cocooned in complete security, left behind her, from the last weeks of her passion, shattering admissions which her horrified sisters toned down in her literary remains. . . . "I am assailed by the worst temptations of atheism." Everything has become questionable, everything is dark. She feels tempted to take only the sheer void for granted. . . . In a situation like this, what is in question is not the sort of thing that one perhaps quarrels about otherwise—the dogma of the Assumption, the proper use of confession—all this becomes absolutely secondary. What is at stake is the whole structure; it is a question of all or nothing. That is the only remaining alternative; nowhere does there seem anything to cling to in this sudden fall. All that can be seen is the bottomless depths of the void into which one is also staring. (Joseph Ratzinger, *Introduction to Christianity*. New York: Herder & Herder, 1970, pp. 17–18.)

And Clifford Geertz notes:

> There is a great deal of skepticism in traditional societies. The inevitable tension which remains between deliverances of common sense and even the most compelling and comprehensive religion assures that, as does the wine employment of religiously based power to less elevated ends. (Clifford Geertz, *Islam Observed*. New Haven: Yale University Press, 1969, p. 101.)

The skeptic, the agnostic, the hypocrite are not necessarily more prevalent today than they were in the past. "Spiritual responsiveness varied then as it varies now; probably just as widely. There was a gap between social ideas and social practice as there is now; probably just as broad. (Ibid., p. 114.)

So if faith cannot be dispensed with today any more easily than it could be in the past, neither was it practiced any more easily in the past than it is today. In Ratzinger's words:

> . . . it is not just today in the specific conditions of our modern situation, that belief or faith is problematical, indeed almost something that seems impossible, but that it has always meant a leap, a somewhat less obvious and less easily recognizable one perhaps, across an infinite gulf, a leap namely out of the tangible world that presses on man from every side. Belief has always had something of an adventurous break or leap about it, because in every age, it represents the risky enterprise of accepting what plainly cannot be seen as the truly real and fundamental. Belief was never simply the attitude obviously corresponding to the whole slant of human life; it has always been a decision calling on the depths of existence, a decision that in every age demanded a turnabout by man that can only be achieved by an effort of will. (p. 25.)

Gilkey, Geertz, Ratzinger all wrote the above passages at a time when we were being assured on all sides that God was dead and that religion was man living as part of contemporary society in the secular city and was beginning to possess the earth, but the optimism of the middle 1960s has collapsed. Science and technology are now in more serious retreat than they have ever been. A non-rational, anti-rational, and at times irrational, "counter culture," stressing emotion, feeling, and sentiment, is doing battle with the rational, scientific, technological culture. Harvey Cox has moved from the *Secular City* to the *Feast of Fools* and is doing his best to persuade the country that he is a harlequin. Hippies, communitarians, astrologers, diviners, witches, are abroad in the land. Educational villages, communes, even (God save us) tribes, are being convened. The transcendent, the Ultimate, and the sacred—albeit frequently in highly bizarre forms—is very much with us once again.[2]

"But something must have changed!" my friend Peter Berger once expostulated to me when we were discussing what he chooses to call "resacralization" and what I choose to call a rediscovery on the part of academics that the sacred is still very much with us. Something has indeed changed, but it's not that faith has become any more difficult or that ignoring the transcendent has become any more easy. Berger, Thomas Luckman, and Clifford Geertz have, each in his own way, put a finger on what has *really changed*: now one must make a choice. In days gone by, interpretive schemes of "meaning

[2] One may well wonder why so many theologians and clergymen gave up on the sacred and the transcendent, not to say on God Himself, so eagerly, before all the returns were in. My own hunch is that a good deal of the explanation can be found in the rather low status that a divinity-school faculty enjoys at the contemporary university, and the desperate longing of faculty and students alike for some kind of "relevance." To achieve this relevance, that is to say, to be accepted by the "really scientific" segments of the university, it was necessary for the divinity-school faculty and students to jettison as quickly as possible anything that seemed to smack of the "mythological" (which of course meant the unscientific). Bishop Robinson's efforts in *Honest to God* are a splendid example of this almost embarrassing haste to assure higher status with colleagues in the "hard" disciplines by a show of rationality, liberalism, and open-mindedness. All this has become even more awkward now. Many of the practitioners of the "hard" and not-so-hard disciplines are having second thoughts about their own activities, and the students of these disciplines are seeking out not "relevant" and "enlightened" clerics, but gurus and holy men.

systems" or, to use a less sociological term, "faiths," were absorbed from our environment as naturally as we absorbed our language, but in the modern world we are free to choose, which means, generally speaking, that we are forced to make a choice. There is not one meaning system, but many. As a matter of fact, faith has become a commodity for which we can shop in the great supermarket of interpretive schemes. It is not that man can dispense with an interpretive scheme, but it is rather that he is now obliged to choose his own or, rather, perhaps, to put his own together from a number of available components.

Some observers—Berger included—will argue that this makes things more difficult for traditional faiths, since now they must compete with other faiths; but I would argue that, at least for the Christian religion, the situation represents a vast improvement. If one must choose a faith, then the faith issue becomes a critical and conscious one, and in an era when the faith issue is a critical, conscious, and open one, when indeed men are obsessed and haunted by the search for meaning, Christianity ought to be confident that it is in an excellent strategic position.

In other words, despite the myth of religionless man, despite the conventional wisdom that modern man is no longer interested in religious questions, I would argue that the very plurality of available meaning systems makes contemporary man far more aware of religious issues—at least, of *real religious issues*—than he has ever been before. Indeed, I would contend that insofar as having to face critical religious questions is concerned, there has never been a more religious age in the whole of human history.[3]

Furthermore, I would argue that it is not merely among the witchcraft covens or the astrology cults or the hippie communes or the

[3] I am sure this assertion will offend all kinds of people, both on the left and on the right, for the left and the right shared the common conviction that religion is falling to pieces. The left considers it good news; the right considers it bad news; and I assert that it is false news. I hope at some time in the future to devote a long study to the question of contemporary religious consciousness. The best treatment of this issue I have seen so far is to be observed in chapters 3 and 4 of Part II of *Naming the Whirlwind*.

great secular universities that man is wrestling with religious issues. The massive suburban professional class has been as badly shaken in its brand of the secular optimistic faith as has academia in its version of the same faith. Despised by the younger clergy as "square" and "middle class," the suburban professionals are inarticulately and awkwardly trying to seek the answers to profound religious questions, more so, if my impressions are correct, than at any time in the past half century. "The good life," as another writer in this issue points out, seems terribly empty if it is not accompanied by "good news."

The point is, then, that man must take a stand; he must plot out for himself a segment of ground from which he can view the ultimate. Even if he decides, with Macbeth, that life is nothing more than "a tale Told by an idiot, filled with sound and fury, Signifying nothing," he still must make a commitment to the notion that all is absurd —a commitment that leaps beyond the evidence every bit as much as the leap to the position described by Teilhard de Chardin when he asserted that "something is afoot in the universe."

Man does not live by bread alone. He requires faith, whether he lives in the twentieth century A.D. or the twentieth century B.C., whether he is a churchgoing Christian or a religionless man whose bible is *The New York Review of Books*. Religion, according to Clifford Geertz, is the "struggle for the real." It is rooted in the "insufficiency of common sense as a total orientation towards life. The events through which we live are forever outrunning the power of our everyday moral, emotional and intellectual concepts to construe them, leaving us, as a Javanese image has put it, 'like water buffalo listening to an orchestra.'" (p. 101.) The media may ignore man's longing for faith, though the flourishing world of psychedelia makes that more difficult; the intelligentsia may discount it, though the horoscopes on the walls of the rooms of the students make that require more effort; the theologians may try to avoid it, though after Langdon Gilkey this will not be easy. As one of my students said when I asked him if he meant that "the God question" was open once again, "Who ever said it was closed?"

I find myself puzzled by the reluctance of Catholics, particularly priests and nuns, to realize that "the enterprise is exploration into God"; perhaps, just having broken out of the constraints of Counter-Reformation Catholicism, they feel that they have to go through a period of enlightenment, rationalism, and agnosticism. Or perhaps it is that the rigid structures of the Counter Reformation protected us from really having to face the God issue, and in the post-Vatican Church many Catholics must face it for the first time. Another way of saying this is that they do not have faith now because they never had faith, at least not faith of the adult variety. Adult faith can only exist when one's faith clearly and decisively answers the ultimate question "Is the really Real absurd and malign, or is it gracious?"

For the Catholic, of course, there is more to the issue than that. The good news asserts not merely that something is afoot in the universe, not merely that the really Real is gracious, but also, the most revolutionary idea in the whole of human history, the really Real is accessible to us. And that is not only good news, but it frequently sounds as though it is too good to be true.

It is therefore much better to be concerned about the peripheral, to argue about birth control, celibacy, collegiality, pastoral councils, future of Catholic schools, election of the Pope, opening the financial records of the diocese, etc., etc., etc. Alternately, it is much better to engage in social action crusades, to march on picket lines, to confront, demonstrate, or, like the brothers Berrigan, to achieve "terrifying moral purity" by going to jail. I do not wish to say that the present controversies in the Church are unimportant. I merely wish to assert that they are worthless if they do not take place in a context of a very conscious and explicit faith about the Real, nor would I want to be counted as an opponent of social action, and if the Berrigan brothers want to achieve "terrifying moral purity," that's their business, but I will assert that Catholic social action that does not take place in the context of the conscious commitment to the nature of the Real can all too easily turn into the same sort of fanaticism as that of Marx or of the contemporary New Left.

One of the ploys we use to escape from the terrifying nature of the good news is to concentrate on the symbols and ignore the Reality that is being symbolized. In Geertz's words, "What sacred symbols do for those to whom they are sacred is to formulate the image of the world's construction and to program for human conduct." Religion is as good as its symbols. "The force of a religion in supporting social values rests on the ability of its symbols to formulate a world view in which those values, as well as the forces opposing their realization, are fundamental ingredients." (p. 97.)

A symbol is not something to be considered merely for its own sake; it reveals something else. "A people's world view is their picture of the way things in sheer actuality are—a concept of nature, of self, and of society. It contains their most comprehensive ideas of order. Religious belief and ritual confront and mutually confirm one another. An ethos is made intellectually reasonable by being shown to represent a way of life. The world view is made emotionally acceptable by being presented as an image of an actual state of affairs of which such a way of life is an authentic expression." (Clifford Geertz, "Ethos, World View, and the Analysis of Sacred Symbols," *Antioch Review*, December 1957, p. 426.)

The temptation in Christianity for a long time, it seems to me, has been to fixate on the sign and to ignore the Reality it signifies, to be terribly concerned about the wording of the symbol and completely unconcerned about the world view and the ethos the symbol conveys, to be deeply involved in controversy about whether its myths are mythological and quite uninvolved in the question of how the world view and ethos as presented by the myths are to be understood and lived in the contemporary world.

To say that the Trinity, the Incarnation, the Gospels, the Eucharist, the Church are symbols or myths is not to deny that they are real in themselves, but it is to assert that they reveal to us more-profound realities, that they are sacraments of the really Real. The doctrine of the presence of God in Jesus, for example, or, to put it in another form, of the Word becoming Flesh, is not an end in itself. The Incarnation is clearly a symbol of the accessibility of the Real and, indeed, of the Real's profound love for us. To fixate on the defense of the doctrine of the Incarnation, namely, that out of love for us God sent His Son to win us salvation, is, I think, to totally distort the meaning of the Incarnation.

To assert that the Word made Flesh is a symbol, a myth, a sign, a sacrament, is not to deny its own reality, not to reduce it to the state of legend or fairy tale, but to say rather that it is a symbol conveying to us the world view and ethos rooted, in Geertz's words, in the very structure of reality.

What is necessary, then, is that we reinvestigate the critical symbols of Christianity, to see what they tell us about the "inherent structure of reality" and about "the way things really are and the way one really ought to live."

In a less self-conscious and explicit age, the symbols would have been enough. It would not have been necessary, save occasionally, to try to probe beyond the symbols to an explicit statement of world view and ethos, but in our day, analytical, critical, and self-conscious and reflective as it is, we must attempt to convert the poetry and the symbols into explicit propositions. In other words, we must try to formulate a creed that makes explicit the Christian conviction about the nature of Reality and the way a good man ought to live.

All the essay, to this point, has been a preparation representing my own version of such a creed. Like all creeds, it is incomplete, inadequate, and, also like all creeds, phrased in the particular language of my own time. Nevertheless, when I assert my belief in God, in Jesus Christ, and in His Church, it seems to me that my commitment to those symbols involves implicitly the acceptance of the following propositions about "the inherent structure of Reality":

1. Love is at the core of the universe.
2. Therefore life triumphs over death, though only by dying itself.
3. Love and life are proclaimed by celebrating.
4. The most appropriate human relationship is friendship, both because it mirrors Love, and because it represents through trust, which is its essence, life's triumph over death by dying itself.
5. The work of Loving Life in the world is moving toward completion. Man's part in this work is to strive that the world may be pervaded by friendship.

6. Wherever men come together in friendship, the Spirit of Loving Life is present in their midst, inspiring them to break out of the bonds of hesitation, doubt, and distrust, in order that they might be for one another.

7. That group of friends who, inspired by the Spirit, seek to proclaim the existence of Love and the triumph of Life through their celebration, and to pervade the world with friendship and joy, is called the Church.

8. Within the Church some men have the special mission of enkindling the Spirit in others, especially by presiding over the celebration of Life and Love.

9. The relationship between man and woman is the model of the depth of love and devotion that ought to exist within the Church.

In most ages of human history, it would not have been necessary to spell out in propositional form the world view behind a set of symbols. The symbols themselves would have been enough to convey that view. But in our reflective and self-conscious age, then, the world view becomes more necessary, though no set of systematic propositions can ever be completely satisfactory. Three principal objections have been aimed at my "mythology of friendship." It has been argued a) that friendship is a weak word to describe the Christian relationship, b) that there is no indication in my "mythology" of the necessity for "the Cross" as part of the Christian life, and c) one cannot find in my summary of the Christian ethos and the Christian world view any sign that a Christian must be deeply involved in the social, political, and human problems of the world in which he lives.

The basic weakness, I think, of these objections comes from a misunderstanding, indeed even a distortion, of the meaning of the word "friendship." A number of people, when hearing my summary, spontaneously remarked, "You're trying to make us Quakers—another Society of Friends." I'm afraid this is a superficially clever remark that misses the whole point. Without intending any disrespect to the Quakers, I must argue that the Quaker meeting does not involve—at least necessarily—what I mean by friendship, and certainly no one could say of the Quaker meeting that the relationship among the "Friends" takes as its model the passion and intimacy and dedication of the relationship between husband and wife.

If friendship sounds like a weak word, I think it is because the reality has been so rarely experienced. Jesus chose at the Last Supper to describe the relationship between Himself and His followers as friendship—a friendship that necessarily involved Him in death for His friends. Jesus' relations with His disciples, in life and in death, in the Resurrection, is anything but the pale, bloodless, casual relationship of mutual tolerance that we often misname friendship. Indeed, I take it that friendship is even a stronger and more difficult reality than "love," as love is normally misunderstood. Even in marriage, where there is such strong motivation and reinforcement for love, if husband and wife are not friends, then they cannot be lovers for very long.

Secondly, to suggest that there is no suffering, no "Cross," in friendship is to betray an abysmal ignorance of what goes on in the friendship relation. Friendship is an emptying of oneself, just as Jesus "emptied" Himself when He became man. The "emptying" in friendship is a death that is a prelude to a resurrection. Friendship is a gift of our self to another, an opening up of our self to pain, rejection, deception, misunderstanding. It is a putting aside of fears and anxiety, suspicion and distrust, and presenting our self, as it were without defenses, to our friend. The gift of friendship can only be offered by one who is confident of his own selfhood. It is not an exercise in search of self-validation, but a manifestation of a self that has already been validated. Jesus was able to "empty" Himself for us because He was confident of Who and What He was. He was able to lay down His life, because He knew He could pick it up again. There is ecstasy in friendship, but also terror.

Revelation is God's communication that friendship is possible among men because it exists between God and men. Men are accessible to each other because God is already accessible to them. From the very beginning, man has yearned for intimacy and friendship. He has always dreamed that affection might be possible. The unique contribution of Christianity is to affirm that God came into the world to call us His friends, and therefore we can be friends one to another.

But friendship, by its very nature, is diffusive of itself. It spills over the boundaries of the friendship relation and seeks to warm all around it. A friendship that closes in on itself, that cuts out the rest of the world, is a counterfeit friendship. Christian friendship is both the root and the sustenance of Christian social action. He who engages in social action in the context of his Christian commitment strives to make trust and affection possible for all men. As long as hunger, misery, ignorance, or oppression stands in the way of friendship, no Christian can be at ease, but, on the other hand, since he is operating out of a context of friendship, there is no room in his social action for hatred, stereotyping, or moral self-righteousness, nor, be it noted, is there any room for quitting when the going gets rough.

It does not seem to me to be possible to claim to be a Christian and not accept these propositions. One might not, of course, like the wording, though the repeated use of the word friendship is surely justified by the New Testament. There are other words—love, life, and the Spirit—but to deny any of these assertions, it seems to me, is to deny an integral part of the good news that Jesus brought. None of the propositions are easy to accept. The Christian faith was not designed to be easy to accept, but let us be clear as to why they are difficult to believe. They are all too good to be true, too revolutionary to be credible, too hopeful to be trusted, too intoxicatingly joyous to be risked.

But that has always been the trouble with Christianity.

4. New Gods—or Old?

A witty divinity-school faculty member—suspected by many to be some relation to the *Christian Century's* Pen-ultimate—commented recently that the secular city was born in Selma and died in Watts. He meant that secularist optimism of the radical theologians could not survive the breakup of the civil rights movement and the emergence of the violent form of black nationalism. It is also rather doubtful that the secular-city model could have survived very long in any case. So while it leaned heavily on sociological categories, it was not willing to face the full implications of either social theory or social research. The secular man may, indeed, exist, particularly on some of the university campuses, or in the skyscrapers of Manhattan Island, but there is no reason to think that he's any more plentiful than he has been in the past, or that he represents the wave of the future.

This is not to say that sociologists themselves have not, on occasion, embraced a fairly simple-minded model of the "desacralization" of man or the "decline of religion." European Catholic sociologists, in particular, are quite fond of speaking of "urbanization" and "secularization," and Brian Wilson's book is certainly the most naive exposition of the secularization hypothesis that one could wish for.

But one need only reread the theoretical works on ritual of

Parsons, Geertz, or Luckman, to say nothing of the article of Shils (in *Ritual and Crisis*, Boston, 1968), and the relevant passages about religion in Durkheim and Weber to realize that the case against the secularization hypothesis on theoretical grounds is quite powerful. Furthermore, empirical research in the United States has not been able to pick up any significant indicators of an increase in "secularization" of the American population. Furthermore, the work of European sociologists such as Martin raise serious questions as to how dereligionized English and Continental populations really are, and how religious they ever were in the past. For example, the survey of the Diocese of St. David in Wales in the early eighteenth century shows that it was a fairly dechristianized locale even at that period, and the French religious geographers can trace low levels of religious practice in France back to the Middle Ages. Secularization is more a function of the social and economic history of an area or a country than it is of modernization.

Peter Berger (in A *Rumor of Angels*, Garden City, 1968) has argued on theoretical grounds that the "plausibility structure" of a believer is threatened when he finds himself in a religiously pluralistic society. However, in fact, it seems that religious denominations are the strongest precisely in those societies that are most likely to be marked by denominational pluralism, leading one to suspect that when the plausibility structure is threatened, the social-psychological reaction is to become more aggressively committed to it, especially when that structure is also the basis for important means of self-identification and social location.

It is, then, in my judgment inaccurate to assume that some of the more recent and bizarre manifestations of religion and the sacred represent a "resacralization." Society was never really "sacralized" in the first place. What we are witnessing, I think, is rather the expansion of Thomas Luckman's "marketplace of interpretive schemes." New forms of the sacred are becoming available in that marketplace, though at least some of them are also very old. These new forms are entering the marketplace precisely for the reason that any other marketplace expands the commodities it is willing to offer—if there is an increased demand for them. The political and social crises of the 1960s, the apparent failure of the liberals' scientific dream, the alienation from traditional faith, both religious and secular, of the younger generation—all of these have raised a demand for new interpretive schemes and new religious communities that can provide meaning and belonging for human life.

We shall speak of three of these "new gods"—two of which are also very old: superstition, ecstasy, and "groupism."

The outburst on college campuses during the past two years of bizarre forms of the sacred is an extraordinarily fascinating phenomenon. Astrology, witchcraft, divination, monasticism, Zen, the White Legion, pentecostalism, spiritualism, and just about any other form of the bizarre of the religious one would care to name, can be found within a stone's throw of the office of almost any agnostic faculty member in the country.

God is dead, but the devil lives.

Young people who engage in such behavior are quite frank about why they do so. They are looking for "experience"; they're looking for something to which to belong; and they are looking, as one young man put it, "for someone in the universe that cares about me." There is something of the "put-on," and not a little of the comic, in such behavior, but also a hesitant attempt to find, as another student put it, "something or someone on which even the IBM 360 must depend." And he added, "Whether I am drafted, whether I go to Vietnam, whether I am killed there or not, all depend on arbitrary decisions by non-human forces. I would like to believe that there is something more than arbitrariness at work."

The tribal gods are being worshipped once again, in substantial part as a protest against the hyperrationalist society and the failures of that society. There are few better ways of rejecting science than turning to astrology, few more effective ways of snubbing the computer than relying on tarot cards, and few better ways of coping with rationalist "liberal" college professors than putting hexes on them.

The second old god is called ecstasy. Whether it be in drugs, rock

music, psychedelic art, contemplation, hippie communes, or pro-
longed periods of fasting, the new initiates are seeking for an experience that will "snatch" them out of the ordinary; they are trying
to establish some sort of communion with the basic and primordial
forces of the universe, even if they have to "blow their minds" to do
so. The *"représentations collectives"* of the summer-end rock festivals
are clearly attempts at group ecstasy. In the immortal words of Timothy Leary, one tunes out in order that one might turn on. Ecstasy,
even drug-induced ecstasy, is, of course, not a new phenomenon in
the human experience, nor, for that matter, is ecstasy induced by
certain musical forms. Indeed, one can probably find direct connec-
tions between some elements of rock music and the ecstatic music
of African religious ceremonies. Nor is the establishment of communities that self-consciously seek ecstatic experience for their membership a new phenomenon. The only really astonishing thing about
the cult of ecstasy is that it seems to be most vigorous precisely
among those young people who are the sons and daughters of proud,
arrogant, secular men who no longer need the sacred or the ecstatic.

The third of the new gods, "groupism," is a little harder to place
in the religious traditions. The desire for open and honest discourse
among human beings is, of course, true of many religious sects of the
past, but the idea that "open" and "honest" relationships become
themselves a religion is, one thinks, something new. Nevertheless,
the immense popularity of T-groups, encounter groups, marathon
groups (clothed or unclothed), affinity groups, communes, educational villages, and other kinds of neotribalism, are sufficient indication that in the post-Freudian world there are many people who
desperately, and at times pathologically, want to find meaning in
group interaction.

Evidence that any of these kinds of group experiences produce
solid emotional growth is, at best, very inconclusive, but they are a
hell of a lot of fun. In fact, many of the claims made for such experiences—that they expand consciousness, provide new insights, en-
large one's life, bring one into a whole "new reality of behavior"—are
not dissimilar from the enthusiastic defenses of marijuana and LSD

by those who are engaged in that particular cult. The "group dynamics" kick seems to be, at least for many of its devotees, merely a somewhat different form of the search for the transcendent. One might even go so far as to say that it's a ritualistic form, because there are certain highly specific phases that sensitivity encounterers are supposed to go through as part of their experience. The leader, or trainer, is the high priest of his group, or congregation; their words and behavior are a ritualistic dance increasingly with the very strong sexual overtones that characterize most ritualistic dances.

These three new religions, two of which are certainly also very old, overlap one another. The neosacralists use sensitivity language, and the mystics and ecstatics form communes and read horoscopes. But they do seem to have certain distinctive elements in each. The neosacralists are explicitly concerned with a transcendent power. The ecstatics want to experience transcendence, but elaborate few theories to explain it. And the "groupists" seek transcendence in human interaction.

But whatever the differences are among these three new gods, there are plenty of common characteristics. They are non-rational, if not explicitly anti-rational. Whatever theories are propounded are simple and elementary; theology and philosophy—as opposed to complex magic—are definitively rejected. One can only find transcendence by breaking out of the bonds of the rationalist world; if necessary, even by "blowing one's mind." On any continuum of Apollonian versus Dionysian religious behavior, the new religions are about as far toward the Dionysian end as one could possibly be.

There are, secondly, Pelagians. Human nature is basically good, at least if it can break away from the trammels of the "square" world. When one is "oneself," then one can do no wrong. As long as one does "one's own thing," one is on the side of virtue, unless, of course, "one's own thing" happens to be recruiting for the CIA or Dow Chemical. While the members of the new religions are only too eager to denounce the sins of the square world, they are convinced that the squares would themselves become virtuous if they shed their "hangups," "turned on," and did "their thing."

Indeed, the Pelagianism of the new religions is fantastically naive; the cynical exploitation of the Haight-Ashbury district and the regressive parent-and-sibling fixations of the hippie communes have done little to shake their Pelagian faith. The new religions "feel" good, no matter what goes wrong.

Furthermore, the new religions are salvationist—that is to say, they preach a way of salvation and preach it with the serene confidence that is only allowed to those who know that they have already been saved. The hippie, the sensitivity enthusiast, the expert with horoscopes, has not the slightest doubt that he has found the answer for himself and for anyone else who has the openness and the good faith to be willing to listen to him.

Therefore, there is something quite *sectarian* about these new faiths. If one possesses not only virtue but salvation, it is then but a short step to decide that one is going to impose salvation upon others, first by vigorous persuasion, and then by force, if necessary. Some of the gurus of the new cults would, one fears, quite understand the viewpoint of the Grand Inquisitor, and indeed, within the Roman Catholic Church, sensitivity training has already become obligatory in certain institutions; these are not inclined particularly to respect the freedom of squares, and the missionary zeal of some of the astrologists is more than a little disconcerting. It is unlikely, to put the matter mildly, that new faiths will ever take over the larger society, but if they do, we had all better be prepared to invest in a good supply of broomsticks and black cats.

The new faiths are *millennialistic*. They can, if given half a chance, create a new world, a world in which everyone is free to do his own thing, to be "up front" in his relationships with his fellows, to be honest, open, and authentic; to "swing," "turn on" and "be with it." Such a millennialistic community, with rock music beating in the background and marijuana smoke drifting over the intense T-group sessions, may seem like a nightmare to those of us who are rationalists or liberals. But, then, most millennial communities in ages past looked more like hell than heaven to those who were not part of them.

The new faiths are *charismatic* both because their leaders, whether they are called "trainers," "gurus," or "chief wizards," are highly charismatic individuals, and also because, implicitly at least, all the members are presumed to have a charisma within them that enables them to "tell it like it is," and to "do their own thing." And among the pentecostals, particularly the rather astonishing phenomenon of Catholic pentecostals, the emphasis on personal charisma is explicit. One cannot escape enjoying the irony of the thought that Catholic pentecostalism seems to have begun in the basement of the Administration Building at the University of Notre Dame.

Finally, the new religions are *liturgical* in the sense that ritual, vestments, sacred instruments, and sacred places and times are of extreme importance, partly because they represent a break with the rationalized, bureaucratized, computerized society which respects none of these values, and partly because liturgy is seen as an avenue to transcendence. Liturgy may be the very simple low-church-ritual Roman Catholic mass celebrated by the priest in his shirtsleeves before a sensitivity session, or the orgy of the Woodstock Rock Festival; but liturgies they both are, and would be seen as such by any anthropologist from another planet who would be so foolish as to get himself involved in either such event.

The new gods, then, are not all that new. Those who worship them, like all religious enthusiasts, think they've found something new. But just as Monsignor Knox's "new sin" didn't really exist, so, one suspects, the "new religion" will never really exist either. The new gods are really the reappearance of the old tribal gods of emotion, superstition, and tribal consciousness. One suspects, for example, that Émile Durkheim would have no trouble in spotting the religious element of an encounter marathon; that it was a *"représentation collective,"* he would not have doubted for a second.

Will the established churches be at all influenced by the return of the tribal gods? Given the speed of communication in American society, and the eagerness of the divinity-school faculty and students to be always in the most avant of avant-gardes, we would be naive to expect otherwise. Rock liturgies, psychedelic vestments, chapels decorated with signs of the zodiac—the interested researcher need only investigate what's going on in the campus ministries to see the determined, if not to say frantic, efforts to reassimilate the tribal gods. Roman Catholicism, of course, continues to have problems keeping up; just at the time when the more avant-garde of the Protestant groups are attempting to resacralize themselves, Catholicism seems to be bent on desacralizing itself. One can only comment in astonishment that the Catholic Church could not have picked a worse time to call into question the cult of St. Christopher.

There are those who argue that this resurgence of non-rational religion is but a temporary phenomenon that will prevail no longer than the secular city. Maybe they're right, though one can only observe that the new faiths now seem quite powerful. They are, to a greater or lesser extent, the result of the disillusionment with the bourgeois, secular, liberal, democratic, scientific society, and the failures of that society during the 1960s to produce peace in the world, justice for blacks, meaningful challenge on the college campus, and authentic friendship among human beings. If the liberal society can recoup its losses, the new faiths may recede, but at the present time such an event does not seem all that likely. Whether a new form of rationalist faith conceding far more to human emotions and sentiments and yearnings for the transcendent than the formal liberal faith—whether such a faith will appear in the immediate future, must remain problematic. The tribal religions, then, while they certainly will never capture a very substantial segment of the population, are likely to be with us. Presumably, sociologists, or at least anthropologists, will want to study them. Some may even join.

5. The Psychedelic and the Sacred

The hippies in the folk-rock opera *Hair* announce the age of *Aquarius*—the new era of peace, love, freedom, and unity they see growing out of the psychedelic movement. Whether the age of Aquarius is about to dawn is a question we can put aside for the moment, though some cynical observers may think that it's rather the age of Leo the Lion that is dawning. My intention in this essay paper is to concentrate more on the present than on the future—to try to understand that dimension of popular and perhaps emergent high culture that we can subsume under the title "psychedelic." I intend to suggest that the psychedelic represents, in part, the resurgence of man's need for the sacred in the face of secularized society. I then propose to make some brief comments on the implications of psychedelia for traditional organized religions.

It is necessary for us to spend rather more time on the definition of terms than one would normally in a presentation such as this, because both terms—psychedelic and sacred—and particularly the latter, are tricky and elusive. By psychedelic, I mean that collection of phenomena associated with hallucinogenic drugs, rock-and-roll music, beat communities, the art of dissociation—be it music, painting, or literature—and the new concern about esoteric oriental religions; psychedelia, in the strict sense, exists only among a relatively small handful of American young and not-so-young people. Fellow travelers of psychedelia, be they teen-agers listening to the Jefferson Airplane, young adults going to Electric Circuses, or college professors wearing turtle-necked shirts and pasting flowers on their Volkswagens (and during the 1968 presidential campaign, flowers with Gene McCarthy's name in them) and talking the language of the hippie community, represent a much larger phenomenon than the hard-core psychedelics. I would also include as at least related to psychedelia, underground films, underground newspapers, and perhaps even the politics of irrational violence advocated by some political commentators (including occasional Catholic editors), and practiced by a handful of alienated young white people.

By the sacred I mean not merely the non-rational, for if I did, my case that the psychedelic represents a quest for the sacred would already be established by definition. Nor do I oppose the sacred merely to this-worldly. The Secular City enthusiasts would have us believe that modern man has rejected the "other-worldly" and intends to find his life satisfactions and challenges entirely in the "this-worldly." Psychedelia clearly refutes such a naive assumption, because it obviously represents a frantic attempt to escape the "this-worldly," to tune out in order that one might turn on. While the "other-worldly" does, indeed, represent an element of the sacred, I intend to convey rather more than this in my use of the word, for by the sacred I mean not only the other-worldly, but also the ecstatic, the transcendental, that which takes man out of himself and puts him in contact with the basic life forces of the universe. This, I argue, is the function of the sacred in any society that sociologists or anthropologists have known, and this, I further argue, is precisely what those who have joined the psychedelic society are aiming for.

Thus, when Tom Wolfe argues in *The Electric Kool-Aid Acid Test* that Ken Kesey and his Merry Pranksters are, in fact, a total religious community, he is, in my judgment, not engaging in mere rhetoric. Kesey and his disciples were engaging in behavior on their trips (whether in a bus or on drugs) that anthropologists of another planet would almost automatically categorize as religious.

At the root of the emergence of the psychedelic is the end of scientific, democratic, secular rationalism and a return to the primordial, instinctual, ecstatic irrationalism that was permitted and even encouraged in most preindustrial societies; the cultural and social organization that has made our economic abundance possible was designed basically to meet the emotional and spiritual needs of Adam Smith's Economic Man. It has succeeded in its goals and, at least by the inhabitants of psychedelia, it has been found wanting for the service of other goals. Its rational, civil, optimistic, individualistic citizen is, from the viewpoint of psychedelia, only half a man, a man caught in the "work-war-wed bag"; man who, as the Beatles put it, lives a dull, routine life.

I'm not suggesting that the society of bourgeois economic rationalism is about to collapse, but I am suggesting that it is in serious trouble; an increasing number of its more sensitive younger members want to have no part of it, and see the madcap irrationalities of psychedelia as a highly desirable alternative.

Let me quote a wide variety of very different observers to sustain this thesis of mine. In reviewing *The Academic Revolution*, by Christopher Jencks and David Riesman, in the June 22, 1968, issue of *The New Republic*, Martin Duberman comments:

> Today's student radicals are far more disenchanted than Jencks and Riesman. Their disgust with traditional procedures is grounded in a growing distrust of rationality itself, of the importance of gathering and transmitting factual information and technical expertise. They are angry because they know that their growth depends on more than the accumulation of information. The kind of growth they value—increased openness to a range of experience, emotional honesty, personal interaction—seems actually threatened and compromised by additional proficiency in the manipulation of ideas and things. In a brilliant article in *The Nation*, Michael Crozier, professor of sociology at the University of Paris, has recently put his finger on the source of current student unrest in this country: it is a rebellion against the new

hyperrationalist world, where the capacity for abstract reasoning is considered the gauge of human worth and the precondition for human happiness. Or, as Berger, one of the hippie heroes of "Hair" succinctly puts it to his teachers: "Screw your logic and reason." The rationalist tradition, as the student rebels see it, has produced a race of deformed human beings, or rather, a race of thinking machines, heads (the old-fashioned kind) without bodies or feelings. The new generation does not wish men to become mindless; they wish them to become something more than minds. Unlike Robespierre, who enthroned reason, these revolutionaries search for a way to topple it.

The most self-consciously esoteric of the rock and roll groups (and to date, probably the wildest, The Doors) is described by Jim Morrison, their vocalist, in *Life*:

> The sound of The Doors is primitive and mystical, the erotic rushes of the organ, the pirouetting of the guitar, the compulsive hide-and-seek of the drums, the dark green lyrics. The music has no meaning, just mood. "Rather than start from the inside," says Morrison, "I start on the outside and reach the mental through the physical." He seeks an unlicensed freedom "to try everything," his mind playing host to angels and devils. He tries to share a catharsis with his audience. . . . He suddenly quotes William Blake: "If the doors of perception were cleansed, man would see things as they are, infinite." Then adds, "We are The Doors, because you go into a strange town, you check into a hotel. Then after you've played your gig, you go back to your room down an endless corridor lined with doors until you get to your own. But when you open the door, you find people inside and you wonder: Am I in the wrong room? Or is this some kind of party?"

Professor Albert Goldman of Columbia observes that the Beatles are gurus, because they "confront their audience with the most basic unbearable truth," that The Doors are shamans, and that The Doors' leader, Morrison, is being particularly shamanistic in the most famous of The Doors' recordings, a Thing called "The End"—a "happening" that concludes in a wild, oedipal fantasy as the singer kills his father and rapes his mother. Goldman also sees the Electric Circus phenomenon as a religious rite in his chapter "The Emergence of Rock," in *New American Review* (ed.) Theodore Solotaroff, published by New American Library, Inc., New York, 1968:

. . . For all of its futuristic magic, the dance hall brings to mind those great painted caves such as Altamira in Spain where prehistoric man practiced his religious rites by dancing before the glowing images of his animal gods.

Magnetized by the crowd, impelled by the relentless pounding beat of the music, one is then drawn out on the floor. Here there is a feeling of total immersion: one is inside the mob, inside the skull, inside the music, which comes from all sides, buffeting the dancers like a powerful surf. Strangest of all, in the midst of this frantic activity, one soon feels supremely alone; and this aloneness produces a giddy sense of freedom, even of exultation. At last one is free to move and act and mime the secret motions of his mind. Everywhere about him are people focused deep within themselves, working to bring to the surface of their bodies their deep-seated erotic fantasies. Their faces are drugged, their heads thrown back, their limbs extended, their bodies dissolving into the arcs of the dance. The erotic intensity becomes so great that one wonders what sustains the frail partition of reserve that prevents the final spilling of this endlessly incited energy.

Goldman may seem to be exaggerating, as may Professor Richard Poirier of Rutgers University in the August 25, 1968, *The New York Times Magazine* when he says of the Beatles:

" 'And the time will come,' it is promised in one of [the Beatles'] songs, 'when you will see we're all one, and life flows on within you and without you.' As an apprehension of artistic, and perhaps of any other kind of placement within living endeavor, this idea is allowable only to the very great."

But it seems safe to assume that such a respectable journal as *The New York Times Magazine* did not think Professor Benjamin De-Mott of Amherst is exaggerating in his analysis of rock music:

But the chief need, perhaps, and there is no sense, incidentally, in pretending that only rock types share it, is relief from significant life-quandaries and guilt. And chief among the quandaries is one that comes down roughly to this: I, an educated man (or adolescent), thoughtful, concerned, liberal, informed, have a fair and rational grasp of the realities of my age—domestic and international problems, public injustices, inward strains that give birth to acts of human meanness. But although I know the problems, and even perhaps the "correct" solutions, I also know that this knowledge of mine lacks potency. My stored head, this kingdom—my pride, my liberalism, my feeling for human complexity—none of this alters the world; it only exhausts me with constant naggings about powerlessness. What can I do?

"Bring along your views," says the rock invitation. "Your liberal opinions. Your knowledge of atrocities committed by numberless power structures of the past. Your analyst's ideas about today's Oedipal hangup. Your own manipulative, categorizing, classifying, S.A.T. braininess. You can not only cross the rock threshold bearing this paraphernalia, you can retreat to it, consult it, any time you want—by turning back into the lyrics. No obligation, in this pop world to mindlessness. . . .

"But now if you'd like something *else*—if you want your freedom, if you'd care to blow your mind, shed those opinions, plunge into self-lessness, into a liberating perception of the uselessness, the unavailing-ness, the futility of the very notion of opinionated personhood, well, it so happens to happen there's something, dig, real helpful here. . . ."

What is being said is that the rock invitation offers the audience a momentary chance to have it both ways: If I accept the invitation, I can simultaneously be political and beyond politics, intellectual and beyond intellectuality, independent and beyond personal independence.

So psychedelia takes man away from the ordinary into the *really Real*, which, as any reader of Mircea Eliade knows, is precisely what religions have always attempted to do—to transcend the finite, ordinary, and confused of their everyday existence and bring man in touch with the basic realities of the universe. Whatever else it may be, psychedelia is a *religious* movement.

I am not, mind you, saying that it is merely a religious movement —it is certainly influenced by the "camp" of homosexuals, by many self-conscious and explicit psychoanalytic concepts, by a certain amount of psychopathology, and also (like everything else in the United States, it is to be feared) by pure economic greed. But after the layers of greed, madness, psychoanalysis, and homosexuality are peeled away, there still is in psychedelia something profoundly religious, and it is, in its own way, a judgment on the failures of the Christian religions of Western society.

Having relied initially on the authority of other observers, let me turn to my own analysis and specify precisely what characteristics of psychedelia are also, in my judgment as a sociologist, characteristics of religious behavior.

First of all, psychedelia is explicitly and consciously an attempt at the ecstatic, whether it be through drugs or music or a combination of the two. As one commentator on rock music puts it, rock can "move people's muscles, bodies, caught up and swaying and moving so that a phrase . . . can actually become your whole body, can sink into your soul on a more-than-cognitive level. Rock, because of the number of senses it can get to (on a dance floor, eyes, ears, nose, mouth and tactile) and the extent to which it can pervade those senses, is really the most advanced art form we have." And as Professor Goldman puts it:

> Like the effect of LSD, that of rock is to spotlight [things] in a field of high concentration and merge them with the spectator in a union that is almost mystical.

The acid head or the rock devotee wishes to escape, tune out, to leave behind the prosaic, dull, "uptight" world of bourgeois society and to achieve union with higher forces as represented by the throbbing rock beat with a marvelous clarity of insight furnished by an acid trip. Psychedelia enables rational industrial man and his children to pull out of themselves, to back from and over against ordinary experience and judge it in the quality of new insight or from the

perspective of new unity. Such have been the goals of ecstatics and
mystics down through the ages, though they have sought their ec-
tasy much less consciously and in most cases much less artificially
than does the psychedelic ecstatic.

Psychedelia is *primordial*, that is to say, prerational when not explicitly anti-rational. It seeks to put aside the hang-ups of organized
society and its conventions in order that it might get in touch with
the profound underlying natural forces in which we are all immersed,
even though the conventions of society cause us to forget this immersion. Psychedelia strives desperately and highly consciously to
be natural (which is probably, one might note, a self-defeating
quest). The new hair styles for both black and white represent, if
in a rather mild fashion, in many instances an attempt, however
pathetic, to achieve naturalness.

Those who know about such things tell us that rock and roll music
results from a marriage of black "rhythm and blues" music with the
"gospel" tradition of black music. In our perspective this marriage
was not an accident. "Rhythm and blues" is a superb manifestation
of black soul—that is to say, the casual, primordial, sensual style that
some blacks have (and that many blacks and many whites would like
to have)—a style that is a ribald rejection of the industrial middle-
class society which has first of all rejected the blacks. Gospel music,
on the other hand, represents an enthusiasm, a vibrancy in religious
devotion, which is also part of the black tradition. Putting the two
together, one produces a combination of sensualism and near-
hysterical enthusiasm which provides the hung-up hyperrationalized
white man with two qualities of behavior—sensuality and enthusiasm—that are dysfunctional in his bureaucratized, formalized, computerized life.

The hippie communities, of course, are another manifestation of
the highly conscious attempt to return to nature—an attempt that
has been well described by Professor Philip Gleason as a new romanticism. Romantic it is, and unsuccessful it probably will be, but
as a judgment on realistic secular society, it is quite effective.

There are, of course, limits to how natural one can be. A friend of mine who is a medical resident of the University of California hospital (near the Haight-Ashbury district) tells me that when hippies show up in the emergency room of the hospital for treatment, they are usually to be found clutching the Blue Cross-Blue Shield cards.

Psychedelia is, or at least attempts to be, *contemplative*. By this I do not mean that it is quiet, for generally it is not, but I do mean that it tries to break through appearances and see *truth* "like it is." Professor DeMott comments, in the August 25, 1968, *The New York Times Magazine*:

> . . . The truth "allowable only to the very great" which Professor Poirier heard in a Beatles song is an explicit assertion of the arbitrariness of ego separations and of the desirability of soaring free from the mind-ridden world of subjects and objects. "I am within you and without you," these sirens call. "I am he as you are he as you are me and we are all together. . . ."

It must be confessed that this particular mystical insight is not terribly original and does not carry the mystical tradition much beyond John of the Cross or Meister Eckhart, to which the psychedelics will reply that while their insight is not new, they perceive truth as not merely on the cognitive level but in the deepest level of their personality. How deep that is, perhaps remains to be seen, but the significant point about the contemplative development in psychedelia is not that it's new, or not even that it's very meaningful, but simply that it is. Mysticism is alive and well and living in San Francisco.

Psychedelia is also *ceremonial*. By this I mean in the present context that it is given to the use of exotic and esoteric symbols—such exotic and esoteric things, that is, as beads and flowers, fancy garments, neck jewelry for men, turtle-necked shirts, Nehru coats, and other such costumes, uniforms, baubles, and trinkets. The Beatles in their nineteenth-century musical-comedy clothes, the Merry Pranksters in their American Flag suits, the flower people with their neck amulets, and even the Hell's Angels in their black leather jackets are, in fact, wearing *vestments*. They have donned uniforms to set themselves off from and over against the Brooks Brothers gray flannel suit. I note, in passing, the supreme irony that precisely at the time that the Roman Church is under pressure to give up vestments, and avoids ceremonies, the world of psychedelia is creating new vestments for its ceremonies, and that precisely at the time the Roman collar is becoming unfashionable, the turtle-necked sweater and the Nehru jacket have become fashionable. Finally, at precisely the time that bishops are under heavy pressure to yield up their beloved pectoral crosses, neck jewelry for men has become the fashionable rage. It's an awfully strange world.

Psychedelia is *ritualistic*. By this I mean not that it has an elaborate system of rubrics that specify in great detail the protocol of behavior, but rather that it achieves its effects through the stylized repetition of sound and action that simultaneously releases the individual from old unions and immerses him in new unities. The whirling of the dervishes, the twisting of the Holy Rollers, the measured cadence of the Gregorian chant, the repetitive dances of the black Africans and American Indians, are all ritualistic. But the ritual was not ritual for its own sake, as it used to be in the rubricized Roman liturgy, but rather ritual for the sake of producing psychological states in which the religious initiate was able to free himself from the controls and rigidities of ordinary life and "break through" (as The Doors put it) "to the other side." While most of the denizens of psychedelia would not think of their behavior as ritualistic, and would surely deny that the "go-go" dance floor has anything to do with the religious ritualistic past, the similarity is unmistakable, and perhaps even a linkage can be traced through gospel music.

The psychedelic is *communitarian*—that is to say, it attempts to create the relationships of everyday living to some kind of concrete and practical application of the insights of mystic union that it has perceived during its shamanistic experiences. Heavy emphasis is placed on being "natural," "outfront," "honest," "authentic," and "spontaneous" in one's human relationships; but such honesty, authenticity, spontaneity, and frankness are often mere self-defeating pretexts for aggression and exploitation, and it's rather beside the point. Psychedelia is repulsed about the artificiality, the phoniness, and the dishonesty of the stylized relationships of bourgeois, industrial, secular society, and tries to create communities of its own motivated by common faith and common love, in which true believers may relate to one another as authentic human beings. Hardly any small religious community in human history has failed to make the same claim. The only thing that makes psychedelia different is that it's equipped with the Freudian and group-dynamics categories and insights, which, while they do not necessarily facilitate one's relationships, at least provide one with the words by which one is enabled to intensely *talk about* human relationships. Nothing about Ken Kesey's Merry Pranksters was more religious than their frequently repeated insistence on being "out front" with one another. Perhaps without realizing it, they were merely striving to respond to the Gospel injunction to say "aye, aye," or "nay, nay" to their brothers and sisters.

Finally, and I am sure it will come as no surprise to anyone, psychedelia is profoundly sexual, as are most religious phenomena. Sex and religion are the two most powerful non-rational forces of the human personality. That they should be linked, and even allied in their battle to overthrow the tyranny of reason, is surprising only to the highly Jansenized Christian who has lost sight of the sexual imagery in his own faith—the intercourse symbol of the candle and the water on Holy Saturday, for example, or the pervasive comparison of the Church to marriage in both the Old and the New Testament.

A good deal of the sexual anarchy of psychedelia can be written off to plain, old-fashioned lust, which operates in the square world, too, but in a more stylized and conventional fashion. However, in addition, psychedelia is dissatisfied with what it takes to be the narrowness, frustration, and joylessness of that relationship of convenience between the sexes called "upper-middle-class marriage," a relationship that keeps man and woman apart for most of their working day, and requires of them commitment in vast areas of concern and interest that are forbidden by very powerful taboos to their part- ners (thus a woman should not be concerned with career, and a husband should not be concerned with child rearing, at least not very much). The psychedelics say, "You squares are hung up on sex; you talk about it, analyze it, worry over it, read books about it, strive mightily to achieve fulfillment with it, but you're too uptight about it to be able to enjoy it. All we do, man, is enjoy it."

On the philosophical level, Norman O. Brown seems to be arguing for the same goal, and the popular novel *The Harrad Experiment* contends that some kind of relaxed sexual polymorphism is not only possible in the bounds of upper-middle-class society, but would make those who are trained for it far more effective in working within that society.

I have argued elsewhere that within the Christian tradition it is necessary to assert that sex must be joyous and playful and that all human relationships are profoundly sexual in origin. The sexual anarchy of the psychedelics or of *The Harrad Experiment,* for that matter, may not be an adequate response to these truths; but the sexual style of middle-class American society—even, one might say, especially among its more enlightened and "liberated" segments—is neither playful nor joyous nor sustaining of a wide variety of healthy human relationships. Sex and faith, sex and mystical union, sex and the primordial forces of the world, sex and ritual—these relationships have been part of the implicit wisdom of most human religions. The failure of contemporary Western religions to remember this wisdom is one of the reasons for the reappearance of the wisdom in the world of psychedelics.

I should like to point out that the ecstatic, primordial, contem- plative, ceremonial, ritualistic, communitarian, and sexual are words that can be predicative of almost any religious *liturgy* that the hu- man race has observed. I am therefore contending not merely that psychedelia is religious, but that it is liturgical, and indeed, a judg- ment upon us for our own past liturgical failures.

In summary, then, psychedelia is a revolt against the superego and against everything in the bourgeois industrial culture of the Western world that smacks of the superego. The reality principle in man has, in liberal industrial society, allied itself almost entirely with the superego. The result is that the transrational, whether it be the suprarational of mysticism and contemplation, or the infrarational of sensualistic orgy, are now in open revolt. Reason cannot rule over the passions and emotions of man as a tyrant, at least not for very long, without running the risk of having an open revolution on its hands. Religion has always been conscious, implicitly, that man is more than mind, that he is also *soma* and *pneuma*—that is to say, both body and spirit—and that while these two characteristics of the human personality seem to be opposed to each other in theory, in fact they are quite closely related and frequently in alliance against prosaic, secular, everyday rationality.

The secular society and most of the religions of that society have simply failed to recognize these facts. They have insisted on treating man as though he were the sober, calculating, individualist of Adam Smith, with perhaps some Freudian sexual instincts added. Reason must govern as a constitutional executive over the passions and emotions, over the infrarational and the suprarational. The scientific world has thought otherwise, and the result is psychedelia. The traditional religions were skeptical of the scientific world, but nonetheless have been so influenced by its Cartesian rationalism that they, too, have lost sight, in practice, of the importance of the infrarational and the suprarational. As regards non-liturgical religions, such as most of the Protestant denominations, there may be some excuse for this, but psychedelia is a particularly harsh judgment on that most liturgical of Christian denominations—the Roman Catholic Church.

While I have tried, in this presentation, to maintain a sympathetic attitude toward psychedelia, I suppose my basic ambivalence has not been altogether repressed, an ambivalence based, at least in part, on the fact that no matter how many times I listen to them, I still think the Beatles are loud, uncouth, and noisy; while I am prepared to concede to the comments of very learned musical scholars that they are important musical innovators, and even that they bear a strong resemblance to Bach, I still prefer to listen to Bach.

While the world of psychedelia represents a powerful critique of modern society, it is, in my judgment, plagued by hang-ups of its own and does not provide much in the way of viable alternatives to that society. It is, first of all, an escape, a loss of nerve, a despair about the Western cultural tradition. The psychedelics have given up; they are, in the fullest sense of the word, alienated. If their alienation is a passing phase, it may be a helpful power to the maturational experience. Alienation as a way of life is, in fact, a form of adolescent fixation. Even if you despair of Western culture and Western society, you are still a prisoner of it; you still live in its context, criticize it in the name of its own values, and define yourself almost entirely in its terms. Alienation has never been a means of human progress in the past, and it is unlikely to be a means in the present. Differentiation and distinction, as square as these activities may seem, are the proper response to our ambiguous, scientific, rational society, since at the present time we can live neither with it nor without it. The psychedelic replies that he does not care about human progress; he does not care about the future; he only cares about his own particular life and the options available to him in that life. It remains to be seen whether a man can have a satisfying or satisfactory life if his only response to the world around him is tuning out and turning on. The monks, of course, went off into the desert, yet they brought the world with them, and somehow or other the desert contributed actively to the world's reform. In any case, given the mass media and the hungry quest for novelty by the squares, the psychedelics are never going to escape from them, particularly since, when the squares take over hippie customs and costumes, even the psychedelics run the risk of being square.

Similarly, it is not evident that the abdication of reason is a tolerable alternative for human living and the tyranny of reason from which the psychedelics are trying to escape. It is a truism by now that the capacity for conceptual thought is what distinguishes man from the other higher apes, but it is not at all clear that the gorilla and the baboon, for example, have developed very superior societies. The very values according to which the psychedelics wish to reject rational society are themselves the product of reasoning. The failure of the hippie communities to have any durability, the failure of the gospel of rock to notably improve even the morality of those who profess it, the failure of LSD and other hallucinogens to produce human beings very much different from those to be observed in squaresville —all these failures suggest that there are no shortcuts to evolutionary breakthrough. Drugs, music, rejection of the most stifling conventions, may be assets to man, the conceptualizing animal, as he struggles toward self-discovery and self-fulfillment, but they do not make any less necessary the use of this power of conceptualization. Acid, rock and roll, and alienated bands of hippies have not contributed much to the solution of the racial problem in this country, the war in Vietnam, the cold war between capitalism and communism, and the barbarism re-emerging in many of the so-called new nations (such as Nigeria); rather than coping with these problems, psychedelia has helped to make them worse, and in this respect it is no different from the square society. Perhaps the demonic in man has been penned up too long and must escape; but if the demonic is released not only from the rigid taboos and conventions of bourgeois industrialism, but also from the guiding supervision of enlightened reason, then it becomes diabolic at very different levels. The popularity of *Rosemary's Baby*, the new adventures into witchcraft that I mentioned earlier, lead one to believe that the diabolic is at least being experimented with. The psychedelics may affirm that God is dead, but it doesn't look like the devil is, and in the meantime we would all be well advised to keep a close eye on our local broomsticks.

Finally, one might say too, that there has been a great deal of nonsense spoken in favor of psychedelia, not the least of it by learned professors. Rock music is an interesting and powerful folk-cultural innovation; the hippie communities are an intriguing development of the beat generation of a decade ago; the hallucinogenic drugs are perhaps an interesting substitute for John Barleycorn; Electric Circuses are, one must admit, something beyond the jam sessions of an earlier period; but that there is here either great musical innovation or notable social experimentation, much less salvation, seems to me very much open to question. Professor DeMott's comment that the future may see "the appearance of a generation so rich in experience of merger and self-transcendence that to its mind Cromwell and Charles and early twenty-first century Harvard sophomores will seem all one" is, one presumes, not meant too seriously. The present younger generation is different from the one that preceded it, but it is not different because of psychedelia; on the contrary, one suspects that psychedelia is the result of the difference in the generations. And given the skepticism of youth about the popular culture of its predecessors, one would be much better advised to speculate that by the end of the present century the acid rock of such groups as The Doors may be as dead as the "big bands" are today. Psychedelia, then, is significant as a symptom of something wrong, rather than as a promising response.

We must, in conclusion, say something about the contribution of the Catholic Church to the problems for which psychedelia is an attempted answer. In a sense, one can say it very briefly. The Catholic Church, the mother of liturgy in Western society, has no response to the problems of the hyperrational society. We have criticized and condemned the modern secularist present world; science, materialism, unaided human reason, secularism, have all been the objects of our heavy artillery, but we have not provided any viable alternatives and have permitted ourselves to be infected by the same juridicism and hyperrationalism that afflicts urban industrial society. And now, irony of ironies, some of our members are beginning to jump on the band wagon of scientific secularism precisely at the time a lot of other people are beginning to get off. At the very time the psychedelics are evolving a new, rich, elaborate, and playful liturgy, we are doing our best to reform ours so that it looks exactly like that kind of Protestant liturgy that was deemed most appropriate for bourgeois industrialism. Neither the Byzantine Solemn High Mass nor the very-low-church Mass of the so-called floating parish is much of a response to hyperrationalism. The hippies are putting on vestments, just as we're taking them off. The psychedelics are seeking ecstasy, and we are having group-discussion homilies. LSD is eagerly seized as a means of creating mystical union, while some of our younger theologians are wondering if, after all, there is any need for prayer. Psychedelia is pursuing the sacred, and we are busy celebrating the glories of the secular city. Once more, we continue at least one quarter of a century ahead of our time—we are answering the questions of 1925 with the solutions of 1950.

We speak of contemplation, and yet we have trained our clergy and religious to be almost pathologically active; we speak of mystical union, but are highly skeptical of anyone who shows mystic tendencies; we praise the glory of ritual, yet we defend, even to the present, ritual reforms that produce not ecstasy, not contemplation, not emotional exultation, but only sleep. We proclaim that Christ came to redeem the physical universe, and we have only just finished warning seminarians about the need for custody of the eyes. We have kept alive the notion of fraternity and community for two millennia, and our fraternities have little community and our communities little fraternity. We claim that the best image to represent our Church is the union between man and woman in marriage, and yet to a world seeking to understand the profound implication of sex for human life while it has not yet put off the shackles of Victorian puritanism, we respond by condemning artificial birth control but by doing practically nothing else to provide a vision of the meaning of sexuality for salvation. The Beatles, The Doors, LSD, the hippies, and all the rest of psychedelia, bag and baggage, are a judgment that God has visited upon his people for their sinfulness.

I do not think the solution of the problem is for a priest to wear psychedelic vestments at Mass, or for bishops to be installed with rock music playing in the background, though God knows, before this decade is over we are likely to see both! (Who knows? It may have happened already.)

Ken Kesey was right. We must go beyond acid, and I suspect that Christianity has an answer, and the name of that answer is joy—joy based on faith and anticipating resurrection. Ladies and gentlemen, I would submit to you that as one looks at American Catholicism today, one sees precious little joy, not much more faith, and little awareness of the coming resurrection. One even suspects that large numbers of our personnel would not be turned on by an LSD trip—not even by a hundred LSD trips—but one would like to think that they could be turned on by the good news of Jesus of Nazareth. Clearly, that hasn't got through to them either.

The picture is not a happy one. Presumably, at some point the Holy Spirit will grow weary of our foolishness and, despite all our efforts, "turn on" the lights of the city set on the mountaintop. But right now, we must pick our way through its darkened streets by the gleam of puny flashlights, while the drums and the bass viol in the background beat ever more loudly. The psychedelic is the crypt of the sacred; acid is a substitute for Christian joyfulness; and rock and roll is a surrogate for faith. In Georges Bernanos' words, we have not got beyond primitive Christianity.

6. The Risks of Community

"My wife and I have just about given up on American society," said the embittered young New Leftist. "A group of people who feel like we do are going to form our own society, live by our own values, and raise our children to believe in the things we believe in. We won't give a damn what goes on in the rest of the world so long as we can be friends with one another in our commune."

"And what," said one of his listeners, "do you intend to do about your Oedipus complexes?"

"We're going to create a society without Oedipus complexes," promptly rejoined the young communitarian.

This rather bizarre interchange symbolizes two fascinating trends in contemporary American society: small, intimate, intense, interpersonal communities—with a quasi-utopian orientation—are multiplying around the country for political, religious, cultural, and psychological goals; but as these communities multiply, an increasing number of observers are becoming aware that, despite the enormous faith and enthusiasm with which such communities begin, most of them seem doomed to frustration because of the built-in dangers of intense personal intimacy.

"Rural" communes are multiplying in the western states—some

observers argue that there are at least five hundred in the state of California, alone. Ken Kesey's fabled Merry Pranksters were apparently just the avant-garde of a new rural communitarianism that will make such historic ideological American communes as Brook Farm and New Harmony look like minor-league efforts.

But the communes can exist in the cities, too, and particularly around university campuses. At some schools, groups made up of younger faculty, students, and an occasional senior faculty member who remembers the glory days of the Young People's Socialist League, find themselves drifting far beyond the original political concerns of the New University Conferences and becoming deeply involved, emotionally, in one another's lives.

Religious communes are appearing, particularly within the Roman Catholic Church, as the traditional parish structure fails to respond to the alleged personal needs of younger and more-intellectual Catholics. In one major urban archdiocese it is estimated that there are over two hundred "underground" parishes, most of them made up of small bands of elite lay people surrounding a priest who, while he may continue in the traditional ministry, is usually fairly disillusioned with its effectiveness and "relevance." Some such communities arise from the cursillo movement, an emotion-filled weekend retreat movement begun in Spain, combining traditional piety with the emotional kicks of a "marathon" weekend. Other such communes or underground parishes have turned to fundamentalism and pentecostalism, complete with the laying on of hands, the speaking in tongues, and the interpretation of tongues. One of the first such pentecostal communes had its early meetings at the University of Notre Dame, which observers thought was an interesting irony for a school that was both the first Catholic multiversity and also still something of a Gibraltar of big-time athletics.

But Catholicism has no monopoly on communes, for underground communities are flourishing in the Protestant, and now even in the Jewish, tradition. On the fringes of Harvard University there has even come into existence an Orthodox Jewish commune, made up of young Orthodox Jews, intending to live a life of religious devotion and doctrinal fellowship.

Nor must one overlook the Zen monasteries, the Meher Baba groups, the intimate fellowship of believers in astrology or the *I Ching*, and other such neosacralist attempts at creating intense interpersonal fellowship.

Finally, a number of educational innovators are beginning to experiment with educational communes—that is to say, small, tightly knit groups of faculty and students in which the learning experience is integrated with a comprehensive set of relationships that affect most of the rest of the life patterns of the participants. "Educational villages" and even "educational tribalism" are phrases that these innovators are fond of using.

When I asked a member of one such experiment how he proposed to cope with the problem of regression to familial behavior patterns, which seems to occur almost inevitably in such communitarian efforts, he looked rather surprised, as though the idea had not occurred to him, and then said thoughtfully, "We won't have just one faculty member in the group; rather, there will be very many, so I don't see why we need to expect that we will have father fixations and sibling rivalries." I suggested that the strongest personality among the faculty members might very readily become such a father figure, and the young man acknowledged that such a problem might indeed arise. However, a colleague responded with almost the same words that I had heard in the conversation reported at the beginning of this article: "Maybe we will be able to create a world without the Oedipus complex."

Most anthropologists and psychoanalysts would be inclined to doubt the possibility of such an event. But that the expectation even exists, is evidence of a profound emotional investment in communitarian adventures, an investment that does not seem to be daunted by the long history of failure in utopian communities. Either such communities become institutionalized—as did the Franciscan religious order—or they vanish in conflict and factionalism, as did Brook

Farm and New Harmony. Yet the communitarian craze persists, and as the astonishing 1960s drew to a close, it seemed to be proliferating at a fantastic rate.

One has a wide variety of possible explanations to choose from when one attempts to assign reasons for the new communitarianism. The impersonality and the corporate irresponsibility of industrial society make men yearn for the simple, straightforward relationships that are assumed to have been characteristic of the peasant past. The artificial, formalized, essentially superficial relationships characteristic of the contemporary world—and even of contemporary marriage—seem pale by comparison with the excitement and warmth of intensely intimate communities. Existentialist and personalist ideologies tell us that we are alone and frustrated, and that we will find meaning only if we find someone to belong to.

But one is permitted to be somewhat skeptical of such explanations. There was not that much openness and warmth in the peasant communes of the past. Nor is there any really convincing evidence that contemporary American suburbs are generating any more loneliness, frustration, or impersonality than other habitats in which man has dwelt. The most basic reason, one suspects, for the new communitarianism is that now man possesses more psychological sophistication—or at least is able to make more-sophisticated use of psychological vocabulary—than in years gone by, and that an affluent society makes it possible for man to push his psychological insights to their ultimate communitarian conclusions.

I am not suggesting that it is merely vocabulary and affluence that are at the root of the communitarian thrust. Men have always yearned for a meaningful intimacy with their fellows; the dialogues of Plato and the romantic poetry of the Middle Ages are but two examples of this quest for intense intimacy. But few men have had the time to spare for such quests, and until Sigmund Freud appeared on the scene, the vocabulary for describing it was hardly operationally effective. We seek more emotional satisfaction, then, at the present time, because we have the time and the money to do so and the categories that enable us to speak somewhat intelligibly about what we are doing.

There is considerable emotional payoff in belonging to a commune—at least as long as it works. One is able "to be oneself"—that is to say, to put aside many of the masks and defense mechanisms that protect the self from the harsh, rationalized world beyond the commune. We can say what we think without any fear of being misunderstood. We can trust others without any fear that they will "chump" us. We can call upon others for close emotional support and expect them to demand of us that we live up to the best that we are. We can create within the commune a new world based on our own convictions and reinforced by the strong love we feel for one another. Excitement in the early phases of a communitarian existence is intense, for the members have found something they had never dreamed possible—warm, close, supportive friendship. It seems indeed to be a pearl of great price. The communitarians have persuaded themselves that they are willing to make whatever sacrifice may be required in order to sustain the at times almost ecstatic joy of communitarian living. But it isn't, as the saying goes, all that easy.

The first mistake that the enthusiastic communitarians make is to overlook the grim historical fact that in any contest between the individual and the community, the community has almost always won. Privacy and individuality are extremely difficult to sustain in any closely knit community. Indeed, privacy and individuality have rarely existed in such communities in the past, and have not, at least according to Bruno Bettelheim, managed to survive very well in the *kibbutzim* of contemporary Israel.

To say that the community triumphs over individuality is merely another way of saying that traditionally the leadership of a community has been able to dominate the other members of the community and to impose norms (generally those prescribed by tradition) on the few members of the community who aspire to be deviant. The new communes have undertaken to establish tribalism by free contract, to produce warmth, intimacy, and social support without the social control and rigidity that have marked close communities in the past. One hopes that the attempt will be successful, but the new "free tribalism" cannot yet be said to be an obvious success.

Furthermore, it is faced with a serious complicating factor: The Grand Inquisitor now knows about group dynamics. He may even be a therapist. It is possible, therefore, at the present time, to manipulate people without realizing it yourself, and without their realizing it. When the year 1984 dawns, Big Brother may turn out to be not a political dictator, but only a T-group trainer.

Manipulation, invasion of privacy, assaults on individuality—all these may be avoided, though with difficulty. But a far more serious danger apparently cannot be avoided: the regression, or transference, problem. The utopian community very quickly takes on something of an atmosphere of a family. The intimate relationships of our childhood with parents and siblings become paradigmatic for adult intimate relationships. One may be able to resist the predisposition to regress to familial patterns, but the predisposition is strong. When faced with new opportunities for intimacy, we tend to fall back on our familial patterns without being conscious that we are doing so. The behavior of our childhood then becomes a paradigm for behavior in the new family, and much of the unresolved conflicts we have experienced with our parents and our siblings are transferred to the new family experience. The leader figure in the community—and every commune seems to have one—promptly becomes a parent figure, and the other members of the commune, brothers and sisters. The membership regresses and fixates at a level of behavior that is scarcely above the infantile. What started out as a new paradise becomes a feuding, fussing, and fighting group of sibling rivals, more concerned about the factions and rivalries that have grown up among themselves than about the ideology that brought the group into existence, or the trusting, loving relationships it was supposed to make possible.

The transference phenomenon, of course, is a standard part of the psychoanalytic process, and as such is extremely useful to the therapist in facilitating the growth of his client. But therapy is not designed to be a permanent intimate friendship. The analyst is able to maintain enough distance from the relationship so that he can interpret the process for his client. But friendship, particularly intimate friendship, is strongly threatened when one partner begins to engage in clinical interpretation of the behavior of another partner. Thus, the tools available to the therapist for breaking out of the transference neurosis are not available to an intimate commune, and vast amounts of psychoanalytic verbalizing about what is happening in the commune does not seem to contribute very much to overcoming the network of infantile and adolescent fixations that now characterize the commune's life.

A therapist may be brought in, but it is an extraordinarily tricky situation with which he is wrestling, for it is not an ordinary therapy group but a closely knit network of would-be friends deeply caught in a transference neurosis. The therapist is almost inevitably a rival of the commune leader. He may be trapped by such rivalry and become as much involved in the transference neurosis as anyone else. The leader now has become *his* father as well as everyone else's, and the other members of the group are his brothers and sisters, who simultaneously hate and love their parent. Or he may successfully replace the leader, only to find that he has become the new father figure himself, but not in a therapy group that meets but once a week and whose relationships do not go beyond that weekly meeting. Rather, he is now caught in precisely the same position as his predecessor. He is the parent figure in a family that expects to relate intimately with one another in many different aspects of their lives. The therapist had better get out while the getting is good.

If the previous paragraphs sound like a description of a process that the author has experienced personally, it is perhaps because they are in part based on such an experience. There is no point in rehearsing the rise, fall, and tentative rebirth of our group; we started out as a discussion and social-action group, became somehow without realizing it an intimate friendship community, and then went through a severe and almost destructive crisis of regression to familial behavior.

Exactly what happened we had best leave to our memoirs, but at least a number of observations can be made on the basis of the experience. Going through it does provide some sort of wisdom, though it is a wisdom that I think we all would agree was purchased at a heavy price.

First of all, one can get caught in a trap before one realizes that it has happened. The conversion from a group of close friends who immensely enjoy each others' company and collaboration, to a neurotic re-creation of everyone's familial past, happens with dramatic speed. Even if the members of the group are sophisticated enough to be aware of the possibility, regression, fixation, and infantile behavior don't feel the way one might think they would. One's friends become siblings or parents almost without warning.

I may be more than a little prejudiced on the subject, but it seems to me that only an extraordinary community leader can avoid being caught in the father-figure booby trap. He must have a strong and powerful sense of his own selfhood and be committed rigorously to refusing to allow his own identity to be violated, especially under the pretext that he is helping other people. Whatever weak links there are in his personality are certain to be exploited by the unconscious forces that swirl around outside him. I am not sure exactly how tough the charismatic figure in the group has to be to survive without getting caught up in unreal and twisted relationship patterns himself, but I can say at least one thing: I was not tough enough, three years ago, to avoid it.

Once the atmosphere of unreality has gripped the group, the personalities of all concerned begin to deteriorate. No one is really himself, but rather becomes a caricature of the weakest dimensions of his personality. Under the strain of the pressure cooker of a group neurosis, everyone dredges up the most unpleasant aspects of his childhood personality. What's more, the relationships among our various childhood selves become remarkably tenacious, and there is no easy way out of them even though we have some vague awareness of what is going on.

While the greatest focus of conversation is on the relationship between the members of the group and the charismatic leader turned surrogate father, the problems of relationships with other members of the group now seen as sibling rivals are, if anything, more important and more difficult to cope with, because they are less likely to be faced. In such a context it is folly to "blame" anyone for what has happened, and yet there is a tremendous need to engage in "blaming" behavior. Analysis and reanalysis of who is responsible for what, and who said what injurious things to whom, in itself becomes one of the most powerful defenses that the neurosis builds up against reality. Furthermore, psychological "talk" readily becomes an excellent means of maintaining the web of unreality, particularly when the members of the group are adept enough in the categories of pop psychology to persuade themselves that they are engaging in honest and open dialogue when, in fact, they are really giving vent to childhood regression feelings.

There is but one way out of such a mess, and that is for the members of the group to acknowledge what, in reality, has happened—that they have all re-created familial relationships in their friendship community. But it is extraordinarily difficult to make this admission; and when the suggestion is offered that collective regression is what is happening, even those who know a good deal about psychology become very anti-psychological: "Other people may have an unconscious that forces them to do things of which they are unaware, but I don't have one. My problems are not in my unconscious at all. They are in you."

If the community, or a segment of it, has been able to acknowledge that regressions to familial patterns have taken place, then it becomes necessary that the various members recognize and acknowledge the contributions their own unconscious needs and drives have made to the network of twisted unreality in which they are caught. Such a step may sound easy, but it is extremely difficult in practice. The group is faced with an awesome decision when it becomes clear that some of its members are willing to admit the neurosis in which they are caught and to analyze their own contributions to it, and others are not. At some point, the decision must be made that those who cannot face the problem and their own emotional investment in it are simply no longer part of the community. They may need help, but the community is incapable of providing that kind of help.

This is a hard saying. It runs against one's sentimentality. As one psychologist who has spent a considerable amount of time studying such groups put it, "It's an eschatological fallacy that assumes that either we will make it together or none of us will make it." Such a brave assertion may sound fair, honest, open, and loyal to one's friends, but it's simply a further form of denying freedom both to those who wish to move ahead (since they are not permitted to do so) and to those who are not interested in or able to face the nature of the problem (since they are continuously submitted to the pressure of those who are). The eschatological fallacy is the last defense of the collective neurosis, and is practiced most skillfully by those members of the group who have the greatest need to control others.

I might note, in passing, that it seems to me that the clergy are particularly likely to get caught in the father-figure trap, since both their religious function and their social role do indeed bestow upon them certain paternal (though not necessarily paternalistic) characteristics. To maintain the authentically mature paternal aspects of one's position (principally by encouraging and comforting), while at the same time not being paternalistic and not permitting oneself to be controlled by the accusation of paternalism, requires, I fear, far more maturity than most of us have.

It is possible for a community to survive the regression neurosis, though, as I said before, only at the cost of great suffering and pain and, in all likelihood, also with the serious risk of losing much of its membership. Considerable growth can take place in the personalities of many members of the group through this experience, but one suspects that there are easier ways of growing.

It is absolutely imperative, once the community has been caught in a network of neurotic familial relationships, that each member maintain the highest respect for himself and the highest respect for others' freedom, even if this freedom means separation. Respect for oneself does not mean arrogance, touchiness, combativeness, or aggression.

Rather, it means an awareness of the goodness of one's own reality and the validity of one's own identity; respect for others' freedom means that one is willing to face reality in such a way that if they choose no longer to walk with you, they are free to go.

I cite this personal example because, from what I've been able to gather about the experience of other communes, it is fairly typical. Human beings experience powerful ambivalencies in the face of intimacy; they are strongly attracted by its seductive warmth, but they are strongly repelled by the fear that they may lose themselves in it. We fall back on the family paradigm for our behavior precisely because it is such a familiar and easy style of action. We know how to do it—we risk little of ourselves in the process. One is willing to put aside defense mechanisms, masks, escapes, barriers, only up to a certain point, and at that point the "other" gets too close. When we become afraid that he will absorb and overwhelm us, then we retreat to our previously preferred defense positions. Most of us are not very good at intimacy and trust, because we do not have enough faith in ourselves to run the risk that these two terrible realities demand. Man has not been conspicuously successful through his long history at overcoming fears of intimacy in his relationship with his mate. Shame, which generally is another name for lack of confidence in one's sexual identity, makes it so very easy for man and woman to fall back on childhood behavior patterns when relating to each other in marriage. Communitarian relationships are analogous to marriage relationships. They are intimate, exciting, challenging, difficult interactions among adults. When faced with the demand for such interactions, our unconscious, and frequently quite conscious, response is to become children once again.

I am therefore profoundly skeptical whenever I read about or hear of a new communitarian venture. It is extraordinarily painful to be caught in the obscure miasma of the regression neurosis, and it is extraordinarily difficult to face the necessity of schism within the community. The pain of separation is not diminished by the observation of one psychiatrist who has spent a considerable amount of time studying such patterns: "When will they forgive you? Some of them may perhaps be reconciled with you on their deathbed—some not even then."

Nor will it help to cite the *kibbutz* in Israel as proof that utopian communities can work. Even if one does not accept Bettelheim's description of what happens to the utopian impulse in the *kibbutz*, one must still note that the original *kibbutzim* had a far stronger ideology and a far more demanding environment than do any contemporary American communities. Whatever their sibling rivalries and parent fixations were, they had to suppress them merely in order to survive, and to some considerable extent, still must do so. Under such circumstances, the crisis of intimacy need not be faced, and in all likelihood has not been faced.

But if any attempts at intimate community must be viewed with skepticism, it does not mean that the efforts should be abandoned. It took us a while to invent the wheel, and fire, too, to say nothing of the lateen sail; mankind, alas, makes progress slowly. Instead of despairing in our quest for community, we should rather be realistic about its prospects. Interpersonal communities seeking intense intimacy are apparently successful, if they are successful at all, only when a majority of the members have a high level of self-awareness and of self-possession, which, be it noted, is different from a high level of ability to verbalize about oneself.

In a convent where I used to say Mass there hung a banner that said, "Community happens!" It does like hell!

7. Leadership in the Church of the Future

A sociologist cannot say anything about the theological nature of Church authority or leadership. When he learns from the exegete and the theologian that the Church indeed must have leadership, he is not surprised, because there is no human organization that can survive for long without leadership. Whether there are some special qualities for ecclesiastical leadership that cannot be found in other human leadership is again a question beyond the scope of the sociologist, but he nevertheless is in a position to say that, insofar as it is a large corporate organization working in the modern world, the Church necessarily has leadership problems similar to those of other large corporate organizations. Indeed, it can be said more strongly: whatever theoretical explanation or justification there may be for leadership, those who occupy leadership positions in large organizations in the modern world have the same kinds of problems, the same kinds of challenges, and must respond with the same sorts of leadership styles.

So the concept of leadership I am going to describe is one that needs not at all to be limited to the Church; quite the contrary, in fact, I would argue that it is one of the missions of the Church, bearing witness to the good news in the contemporary world, to lead the way in developing patterns of leadership that are appropriate both to the problems of our highly complex society and to the deep yearnings of the human personality for meaningful relationships in the midst of large corporate structures. The Church's leadership style should be a light shining on the mountaintop to show other large corporate organizations that leadership can be effective and, at the same time, humane. Professor John Schaar describes the kind of human leadership (as opposed to bureaucratic) that is demanded both by the militant personalism of the New Left and by the requisites of effective organizational functioning:

Humanly significant leadership bases its claim to authority on a kind of knowledge which includes intuition, insight, and vision as indispensable elements. The leader strives to grasp and to communicate the essence of a situation in one organic and comprehensive conception. He conjoins elements which the analytic mind keeps tidily separate. He unites the normative with the empirical, and promiscuously mixes both with the moral and the esthetic. The radical distinction between subjective and objective is unknown in this kind of knowledge, for everything is personal and comes from within the prepared consciousness of the knower, who is simultaneously believer and actor. When it is about men, this kind of knowledge is again personal. It strives to see within the self and along with other selves. It is knowledge of character and destiny. . . .

The language in which the knowledge appropriate to humanly significant leadership is expressed is also very different from the language of rational and objective discourse. It is a language profuse in illustration and anecdote, and rich in metaphor whose sources are the human body and the dramas of action and responsibility. This language is suggestive and alluring, pregnant, evocative—in all ways the opposite of the linear, constricted, jargonized discourse which is the ideal of objective communication. Decisions and recommendations are often expressed in parables and visions whose meanings are hidden to outsiders but translucent to those who have eyes to see. Teaching in this language is done mainly by story, example, and metaphor—modes of discourse which can probe depths of personal being inaccessible to objective and managerial discourse. Compare the Sermon on the

Mount with the latest communiqué from the Office of Economic Opportunity in the War on Poverty, or Lincoln's Second Inaugural with Nixon's first. (John H. Schaar, "Reflections on Authority," *New American Review*, Vol. 8, 1970, pp. 75–77, 78.)

Though Professor Schaar obviously did not have the Church specifically in mind, one still is forced to say that his description is an excellent description of what leadership should be like in the Church —and of what it was like in the New Testament.

I also wish to note that the kind of leadership I will describe is required of *all* levels of large corporate organizations, not merely at the top. We can have leadership that is friendship in the papacy; we will have it in the hierarchy when we have it in the clergy. The strange propensity to expect those above us to lead in a way we do not is necessarily a barrier to reform and renewal, and the demands of the human personality, as well as the requirements of organizational effectiveness, necessitate the kind of leadership I will describe, wherever leadership is to be exercised in the Church.

It is increasingly obvious that the critical positions in modern society are occupied not by individuals, but by decision-making teams, since no individual can expect to have the information or expertise necessary to cope with the complex problems that he must face in a decision-making capacity. If these decision-making teams are going to be successful, they must be composed of friends, that is to say, men who have trust, affection, and respect for one another. This is not an option; it is not something that is desirable because it is pleasant or virtuous; it is a functional necessity. The leader of a decision-making team—and thus the critical person in a large modern organization— is a man who facilitates friendship among his colleagues and presides over it.

Let it be noted carefully what Schaar is saying. He is insisting not merely that this is a humanly desirable kind of leadership, but that it is functionally necessary if large corporate structures (government, business, labor, education, and church) are not going to become monstrous machines running out of control. Schaar thinks there is a third choice, between Abbie Hoffman and Robert McNamara, but let it be noted that the third alternative is not one for which many models exist. I do not think it is too unrealistic to demand that a church whose Founder claimed that leadership was friendship, be in the avant-garde in developing such a model.

I now wish to turn to a more detailed description of what I take to be the functions of leadership in the Church, or indeed, in any human organization.

In an article in *Commentary*, Midge Dichter suggested that it was reactionary to wish to be governed by attractive people, and deduced that the whole Kennedy cult of the 1960s was basically reactionary. This is the sort of superficial smartness that one has come to expect from intellectual journals. Reactionary or not, the human need for leaders who incarnate the goals, values, and élan of an organization is powerful and probably permanent. An effective leader must be "transparent." That is to say, his commitment to the values and goals of the organization must be such that the members can see in him the personification of what the organization is striving for. What is required, one suspects, is not a special kind of personal attractiveness, but rather a clear, enthusiastic, and articulate commitment to goals. The great men of the sixties, such as John Kennedy and Martin Luther King, were not pied pipers, but they were men whose convictions and commitments were unmistakable. Man seems to need in his leaders evidence that they "really believe" the things they say and that they really have confidence that the goals they describe can be achieved. I do not believe that the mass media can "merchandise" this quality.

There is no room, then, in the symbolic leader for self-pity or hand-wringing, for indecisiveness or hedging of bets. He must have courage, wit, hope, and the willingness to take risks. He must be able to channel energies and enthusiasms instead of trying to restrain them. He must, in John Kennedy's words, say, "Why not?" instead of "Why?" Midge Dichter to the contrary notwithstanding, it seems most unlikely that either the need for or the availability of this sort of leader is going to be eliminated from modern society.

The symbolic leader plays both a prophetic and a therapeutic role, which is to say, he both challenges and comforts. He stirs his followers out of their lethargy, complacency, and self-satisfaction. He is not satisfied with the way things are, and he demands of those associated with him that they use the best of their talents. On the other hand, he is not a prophet in the sense of Amos denouncing or Jeremiah sitting on the edge of the city calling down imprecations. He is also able to comfort, to reassure, to strengthen, to support. If he says to his followers that certain things must be done, he also says they are capable of doing them. His prophecy is never such as to make his associates feel inadequate. Quite the contrary, his prophecy is designed to make them feel more adequate than they were before they heard the prophecy.

Precisely because he is in a leadership position, the leader is forced to see the "big picture"; that is to say, he must be aware of both the over-all needs of his organization and of the values and traditions that constitute the ideology of the organization. His associates are involved in their own specific tasks and needs, and are not normally inclined to look beyond these immediate tasks and needs to the "big picture." It is a leader's role, then, precisely to prevent his associates' turning in on themselves and their own immediate problems and preoccupations. He is *not* a man who provides answers—a relatively easy and quite futile task. He is rather a man whose task it is to ask the right questions, to point out the relationships between the group's values and the "big picture," which will force the other members of the group to think through their beliefs and their obligations. He poses problems, not solutions.

And he also rejects incomplete answers, that is to say, answers that do not take into account either the ideology of the organization or the reality of the problems it faces. Thus, the Kennedys rejected an answer to the Cuban missile crisis that would have involved a surprise attack on Cuba, precisely because it was false to the American tradition. Similarly, one would suppose that a religious leader would reject any response to contemporary problems of sexuality that would ignore the need to respect human life. But what I am suggesting is that the leader would ask the question: "What does our insight into the meaning of sexuality imply for our religious beliefs and behavior?" and let his colleagues attempt to arrive at an answer instead of imposing one on his own initiative. It takes no great skill to provide answers, but to ask the right questions and to distinguish between answers that are adequate and answers that are inadequate, require a great deal of skill. Unfortunately, we do not yet seem to have much of this skill in the Roman Church.

The leader realizes that in the complex world in which we live he can ill afford to lose any of the talents of the members of his group. He therefore must create an atmosphere in which there is the greatest possibility for his individual colleagues to develop their talents to the maximum. This means not only guaranteeing them the greatest degree of freedom possible within the group but also creating an atmosphere of harmony and social support among his colleagues. Basic to this, of course, is his obligation to protect the rights of members of the group, but also he must do all that he can to see that the conflicts and the strains that exist among his various colleagues are honestly and openly worked out. Conflict and tension cannot be eliminated from the human condition, but their negative effects can be minimized both by bringing conflicts into the open and by providing for everyone a sufficient amount of personal security so that every new conflict does not seem to be an attack on the core of one's personality.

The interpersonal skills that are required of the leader might be compared to the socioemotional role traditionally attributed to the mother of the family, for it has been assumed that the mother is the one who has been responsible for harmonizing difficulties, healing hurts, protecting rights, and facilitating in development of talent. I would note, however, that in the best of modern families the father shares in the socioemotional leadership just as a mother shares in the task-oriented leadership.

Despite the naive romanticism of our young, and some of our not so young, no groups of human beings can function for very long unless there is organizational effort. The leader then either must be an administrator or see that administration gets done. Administration may be less important than symbolizing the goals and values in an organization or interpreting its ideology or creating an effective interpersonal environment. This does not mean that it is unimportant. Because some ecclesiastical leaders have, alas, equated administration with leadership, does not mean that we can now have ecclesiastical groups in which administration is taboo.

The leader must, first of all, obtain the consent of his colleagues for the major decisions that the group makes. Effective authority is, in the final analysis, the ability to obtain consent. Just as it is easy to give answers, so it is easy to give orders. But orders and answers can be ignored, particularly when one does not have a secular arm available to enforce them. However divine one may be persuaded one's power is, it still is a useless power unless it is accepted by those toward whom it is being directed. A leader who is not able to obtain the consent of a very large majority of his colleagues on a given policy matter has failed as a leader, no matter how noble the title he may claim. Not only, then, does the leader propose the right questions, but he also presides over the dialogue that will lead to a response to the questions. He realizes that everyone whose co-operation is necessary for the implementation of the decision ought to have some kind of participation in the making of the decision. If any substantial part of the membership is excluded from the decision-making, then the chances of a successful implementation of the decision are minimal.

Secondly, the leader must preside over the implementation of the decision. He must direct and co-ordinate the activities of his colleagues in such a way that the maximum result is obtained with the minimum of effort. It is not, for example, necessary to convene a meeting of the whole group to determine whether stamps should be purchased (not, as happened in one convent I know, have a twenty-minute discussion each day before Mass as to what hymns were to be sung). The leader must see, in other words, to the "bookkeeping" and "housekeeping" details. It is an onerous and perhaps thankless task, and his colleagues may grumble and complain about the need to be concerned over such details. Nevertheless, they would grumble and complain much louder if the leader failed to arrange for the bookkeeping and the housekeeping in such a way that the organizational climate of the group did not provide some stability and order.

Finally, the leader must see that the organization is arranged in such a way as to maximize pluriformity among the various subgroups within it. For just as the talents of the individuals are developed when they have the greatest possible amount of freedom, so the contribution of subgroups will be most effective when they, too, enjoy the greatest amount possible of initiative, responsibility, and structural flexibility. Just as it would be disastrous for an organization if everybody behaved exactly the same, so it would be disastrous if each subgroup within the organization were under obligation to follow one, and only one, model. Pluriformity is messy, inconvenient, and fits poorly on an organizational chart, but in its absence, vitality and variety and ingenuity and creativity vanish. Perhaps the worst thing about Max Weber's bureaucrats is that they are so uniform. Given the strain toward routinization and uniformity in the modern world, the leader preserves pluriformity only if he is willing to take positive action to promote, facilitate, and guarantee variety and flexibility. He cannot assume, at least not in the present stage in the evolution of the species, that pluriformity will take care of itself, but he can assume that the alternative to pluriformity is apathy.

The style and degree, the depth and quality, of friendship in human organizations will vary from organization to organization. Presumably, in a church that argues that love beats at the core of the universe, and that union among its members ought to be as intimate as the union between husband and wife or between vine and branches or between head and body, the depth of friendship required between the leader and his associates ought to be very great indeed. That we have not achieved such a combination of leadership and friendship is not a proof that the ideal has been tried and found wanting, but as Gilbert Chesterton has said, "It has been found hard and not tried."

Yves Congar has suggested to me that the kind of leadership of which I am speaking is a kind of leadership of paternity and fraternity. The leader, in my model, obviously plays some paternal (though not paternalistic) roles. He encourages, he exhorts, he challenges, he questions, he demands, he organizes. Yet, if there is a paternity involved, it is a paternity of someone who realizes that he is dealing with people who are his equals and his colleagues and, more than that, his brothers. They are not children to be directed whither he will. They are rather colleagues who, together with him, jointly determine the direction of the groups. The friend who is a leader, the father who is a brother, must see himself as a catalyst rather than a ruler. I would merely argue that in being a catalyst there is a strong dimension of paternity as well as fraternity.

Herein, of course, is one of the very considerable dangers of leadership. The need for strong, vigorous, *paternalistic* father figures whom we can both lean on and hate is still very great in contemporary society. The leader is indeed strong, vigorous, challenging, and prophetic, but his resolute refusal to be paternalistic, to make other peoples' decisions for them, to provide rigid structures and ready-made answers, will create serious anxiety in many of his colleagues. Whatever they may say verbally, they want a father, and not a father who is a brother. The leader's refusal to fulfill the total father-figure role will lead some of his colleagues to hate him far more vigorously and far more openly than if he were a traditional parent surrogate. Indeed, there may even be a strong positive correlation between their charges that he is trying to dominate and manipulate them and his stern refusal to be authoritarian. One of the reasons that the kind of leadership I am describing is having such a difficult time emerging in modern corporate organizations is precisely that those who need strong, domineering, inflexible, and authoritarian leaders are not willing to permit it to emerge despite all their claims to the contrary.

I think it is all too obvious that we do not have much of this sort of leadership in the Church, but it also ought to be obvious that the bright vision of the Second Vatican Council and of Cardinal Suenens' interview on coresponsibility will never be achieved unless we have more such leadership. Let me point out very carefully that I think that such leadership is required at all levels—the papacy, the hierarchy, the pastorate, and the various new free associations that are beginning to emerge. I would suggest that perhaps the best way to facilitate the emergence of such leadership is not to criticize those above us for not practicing it, but, rather, determine whether we practice it ourselves.

I take it that one of the principal themes of the Christian message is that God is accessible to men and that, therefore, men are accessible to one another. Love among men becomes possible when it is seen with God, Who loves men. We became absolutely convinced that we could be friends with one another when Jesus told us that we were His friends and He was our friend. But if friendship among men is possible, then its possibility should be most obviously manifest in the relationships within the Church. And if leadership and friendship can be combined—as they were in the New Testament—then this combination should be most obvious in the Church. We therefore must develop models of leadership, both because the world needs to see these models and because our own tradition, particularly as symbolized in the relationship between Jesus and His followers, requires it of us. These models are far more important than experimentation with ecclesiastical structures done in the absence of such clear models. I am personally convinced, for example, of the necessity for electing bishops by the clergy and the people of their dioceses, and electing them for limited terms. I am also convinced that the method of electing the Pope should be notably changed so a far more representative body might have the awesome responsibility of selecting the leader of the Church. I am finally convinced that while our leaders are elected, and elected for terms, they still should have strong, powerful positions, for it is only strong leadership that makes democracy possible. In weak leadership, democracy turns into either anarchy or tyranny. I further do not think it is possible for the kind of leadership I describe to emerge in the absence of such structural change. The present method of selecting ecclesiastical leadership makes it extraordinarily difficult for the leader to be a friend. Nevertheless, I am convinced that modifying the nature of the selection of leadership will not be enough if we have not thought through more clearly than we have thus far. If we want our leaders to do, what kind of men ought they to be? Do they have the resources of faith and of strength, conviction and hope, spirit and courage, to repeat the Gospel statement: "I do not call you servants; I call you friends."

PART II
American Catholicism

8.   American Catholicism 1950 to 1980

INTRODUCTION

Since Father John Carroll, S.J., returned from France to the United States in 1775 firmly persuaded that with the suppression of the Society of Jesus in France his life work was over, it has been argued that Catholicism in the United States has been in transition. The history of the American Church, as the history of any major institution in the modern world, is nothing more than a long series of transitional experiences. And yet, as we look back on the decade just ended, we must admit that American Catholicism has gone through a dramatic, profound, and at times astonishing, transition.

But if one is to talk about the 1960s, one must also say something about the 1950s. The underlying causes of what we can only call the explosion in American Catholicism were evident enough even in the 1950s—though it must be confessed that none of us managed to see them. Finally, we shall also engage in the sociologist's favorite trick of donning the prophet's mantle, and project the changes of the 1960s a decade hence and try to imagine what American Catholicism will look like four years before George Orwell's fateful date of January 1, 1984.

Two incidents that occurred in my life a decade ago will give some notion of the magnitude of changes of the past decade. In the summer of 1959, I was asked to address the National Catholic Liturgical Conference at the University of Notre Dame on the subject of "Liturgical Change." Two weeks before the conference began, I received a note saying that since, for the first time in the history of the conference, members of the hierarchy were to be officially present, it was advisable that we be very careful about what we would say in our presentations. We were urged not to mention the possibility of vernacular liturgy, because this was certain to offend the hierarchy. Cautious, careful young man that I was, I had no intention of mentioning the vernacular. Within the next decade, however, the same bishops in whose presence the vernacular could not even be mentioned, had authorized Mass that was totally in English and represented the most dramatic liturgical changes in twenty centuries.

Secondly, in September of 1960, when I rather gingerly approached the Sociology Department of the University of Chicago, the number of Roman Catholic priests on campus could easily have been gathered in the dining room of the Catholic Students Center. Father Thomas McDonnaugh, the chaplain, had a yearly dinner for the ten or twelve clerics who were braving the pagan wilderness of William Rainey Harper's university. A decade later, there are more priests and nuns on the campus of the University of Chicago than anyone can estimate. The Psychology Department, with some embarrassment, suggests that it would be nice if priests did not wear their Roman collars to class, because it turns out that in some of the classes the majority of the students are Catholic clergy (most of them Jesuits). The pious agnostics at the University of Chicago must shake their heads in dismay: it is a mistake to let one or two Catholics in, because before you know it, they try to take over the place; and the trouble is that all Catholics look alike . . .

THE 1950S

I intend to use the concepts of "culture" and "structure" as tools to organize my interpretation of the phenomenon of contemporary

American Catholicism. The model that can be created by the use of these tools is not necessarily the only model useful for reflecting on the American Church, but it is one that we sociologists rather like to use, and it does enable us to make some cautious projections about what the next decade may hold. I can promise the reader, however, that he will not be excessively burdened by sociological jargon. By "culture" I mean the "values," "beliefs," "norms," and "folkways" of a given collectivity or subcollectivity of human beings. By "structure" I mean the more or less established pattern of interaction among the numbers of the collectivity. The local parish, then, is an ecclesiastical "structure" or "institution." The belief that the pastor is the unquestioned head of the parish is part of the culture of the collectivity, or one of its values.

William Ogburn introduced several decades ago the concept of a "cultural lag." He argued that human institutions do not change as quickly as do human values. Many of the conflicts in a society can be explained by the fact that change in structure lags behind change in culture. Thus, the values of American society on matters of racial justice have changed more rapidly than have the patterns of interaction that constitute the structure of American society.

Professor Talcott Parsons and his disciples have added the notion of "system" to the cultural-lag theory, and point out that while in some instances structure does indeed lag behind culture, in yet other instances cultural changes lag behind structural changes. Thus, for example, Professor Clifford Geertz has demonstrated how Javanese religious values have not changed as fast as the structure of the society. Hence, these values frequently create conflict in that social structure. In other words, values and institutions can frequently get out of kilter with one another, as one or another moves more rapidly. In addition, Parsons notes that in our society there are a number of different value systems and institutional orders interacting with one another in various fashions. If one considers Roman Catholicism in the United States as a subsystem of a larger social system in this American society, one can see that the influence of the larger society and its structure and culture on the structure and culture of Catholicism provides a number of opportunities for a delicate balance between the two within Catholicism to be put in jeopardy.

We will contend, then, that the following processes have occurred:

1. The values of the larger American society increasingly impinged on the values of American Catholicism. The institutional structure of the Church was not able to cope with this dramatic confrontation of values, particularly when it was aggravated by the dramatic changes in the universal Church at the Second Vatican Council.

2. A substantial number of American Catholics, particularly in the various elite groups, then became unwilling to concede legitimacy to the old institutions. The new values that brought the old institutions down proved incapable of generating new values or relationships; hence, this created a crisis in structure which then produced an even greater crisis in values.

Or to put the matter somewhat more concretely, American Catholicism could not cope with the new ideas that began to surge during the 1960s. As the old values faded and the old structures crumbled, even those who had introduced the new values were not especially sure of themselves or in what direction they were both going. American Catholicism is, then, in a double crisis, with both beliefs and organizational patterns in great disarray.

We must note here, however, that disarray is limited to what we must call elite groups within the population—principally the clergy, the religious, and those laity who are willing to devote considerable concern to the goals and activities of the Church. As we shall point out later, there is no evidence that the overwhelming masses of the Catholic population have been notably affected by the present crisis —at least not so far.

Enough for sociological framework. Let us now turn to the Catholicism of the 1950s. To an outside observer, American Catholicism in the 1950s looked remarkably vigorous. In the years since the Second World War, Catholics had made enormous social and economic strides. Data collected in 1957 showed that the Catholic population had drawn even with the rest of the American population, both socially and economically. A Catholic had almost been nominated for the vice-presidency in 1956, and there was some chance of his running for the presidency in 1960. Catholic schools had doubled their proportion of the student population (from 6 to 12 per cent) since the beginning of the Second World War, and enrollment in Catholic colleges was increasing dramatically. The number of priests and nuns was also increasing, and toward the end of the fifties there was a major leap forward in religious vocations, apparently because of the coming of age of babies born at the beginning of the Second World War.

There were no challenges to the sexual mores. Teachings on birth control and divorce were still unquestioned by devout Catholics. The liberal and progressive Catholic action movements, such as the Christian Family Movement and the Cana Conference, all too easily became fertility cults. The press and the other forms of mass media, particularly in large cities, were very wary of putting out any kind of news that could be interpreted as being critical of the Church. Defections from the priesthood and the religious life were expectably rare. A greater proportion of Catholics went to church and received Communion in the United States than any major industrial country in the Western world. While there were some defections from Catholicism, these were easily made up by the very substantial number of converts that were won to the church each year. Auxiliary agencies such as Catholic newspapers, magazines, religious-goods and book stores, and publishing houses were flourishing.

One can scarcely believe that that was only a decade ago. Enrollment in Catholic schools has dropped dramatically. The convert rate has also gone down, but there are more priests than there were in 1960. Vocations to the priesthood and the religious life seem to be drying up, and perhaps as many as 10 percent of the priests in the country have left the priesthood, as has indeed one bishop. The new independent Catholic press engages in vigorous criticism of the Church. Every internal conflict of any importance becomes front-page news in the secular journals. Authority no longer demands instant respect. The Church's teaching on birth control is openly flouted by a vast majority of the laity and a substantial majority of the clergy. Many parish priests do not hesitate to admit to the sacraments people who have remarried after divorce. Liturgical innovation abounds—including cocktail party masses (with whiskey and ry-Krisp used instead of bread and wine) and psychedelic worship; "underground" ecclesiastical communities existing independently of, if not in open schism from, the institutional Church are rapidly increasing. Priests' unions and associations have sprung up to engage in collective bargaining with bishops. Mass attendance has declined somewhat, and auxiliary agencies such as magazines, newspapers, and religious-goods stores and publishing houses are fast vanishing from the scene. American Catholicism has been turned into a disaster area.

The raw statistics (Table 1)[1] for American Catholicism between 1949 and 1969 begin to give a hint of some of the changes that have occurred. There are more priests in 1969 than there were in 1949, and somewhat more nuns in 1969 than in 1959 (though not very many). But there has been a decline of seminarians between 1959 and 1969 and a dramatic decline in converts. Enrollment in colleges and secondary schools is up, but enrollment in elementary schools is down. Table 1 seems to suggest that 1959 represented the top of an inverted U curve for a number of indicators for growth of the Catholic population. Since 1959 the curve has begun to go down.

But the trouble with the statistics in the country directory presented in Table 1 is that Table 1 does not take into account changes in the size of the Catholic population, nor changes in the age structure of the whole American population. Surely there are more priests in 1969 than there were in either 1959 or 1949. But the adult population is much larger in 1969 than it was in 1959, and furthermore, the proportion of young people in the population has dramatically increased in the past two decades. In Tables 2 and 3[2] we try to take into account the increased size of the population and its changing age structure. We ask in Table 2, for example, what the relative in-

[1] See supplement, p. 164.
[2] See supplement, p. 165.

crease or decrease in Catholic population statistics was in 1959 and 1969, assuming 1949 as a base year; thus the first figure in column one of Table 2 indicates that in 1959 there were more than five thousand more priests than were necessary to maintain the ratio between priests and adult population that existed in 1949. Column one also indicates that there were more than six hundred thousand more elementary school children in the Catholic population in Catholic schools in 1959 than would have been necessary to have the increase in elementary school enrollment in Catholic schools maintain parity with the increased enrollment in public elementary schools.

Table 2 indicates quite clearly that the decade between 1949 and 1959 was a time of not only dramatic absolute increase in Catholic population indicators, but also a very considerable relative increase. On the other hand, it also shows that the relative decrease between 1959 and 1969 was far more striking than the absolute decrease.

Table 3 assumes 1959 proportions and asks what the relative changes were between 1959 and 1969. Here the figures are quite striking. There are more than fourteen thousand fewer sisters than there were in 1959, almost sixteen thousand fewer seminarians, and almost three hundred thousand fewer grammer school students. Only secondary education and colleges have shown relative increases between 1959 and 1969. Tables 2 and 3 indicate, therefore, that the decade between 1959 and 1969 was a decade of dramatic loss for American Catholicism, a loss that is hidden in the raw statistics of Table 1 by the changing age structure of the population. Statistically speaking, Catholicism made immense progress in the decade ending in 1959 and suffered serious losses between 1959 and 1969. Indeed, as far as sisters, seminarians, and converts are concerned, the relative position of the indicators in 1969 is worse than it was in 1949 (and elementary education barely holds its own in the two decades). Given the decline in seminarians, one can also predict that by 1979 the number of priests will also, relatively speaking, be substantially lower than it was in 1949. Not only, then, did the 1960s wipe out the gains of the 1950s, but in many respects they left Catholicism in a worse state than in the 1940s.

American Catholicism is in deep trouble. If the statistical trends described in the Tables cannot be reversed, then the long-range outlook for American Catholicism is a gloomy one.

There will be those who argue that what I have described is not in fact disaster, but actually, from the religious viewpoint, a sign of great growth. They will contend that the destruction of old and outmoded institutions is progress, and not a portent of gloom. In terms of sociological analysis, I am unable to respond to them. They may, very well be right. My only point is that that collectivity which I would have described in the 1950s as American Catholicism is going through an experience that, by the objective standards of social science, looks very much like deterioration. Something new and better may emerge if this deterioration is permitted to go on to its logical conclusion. But the something "new and better" is likely to bear little resemblance to the Catholicism we knew in the 1950s; it may also, in the final analysis, not turn out to be "new and better," even by the standards of those who eagerly await its arrival. But in any case, our concern is with the human institution that is commonly called the Roman Catholic Church of the United States. We shall leave to others, more theologically sophisticated, discussions of whether the demise of that institution is a good thing or a bad thing. Our question must rather be with why it seems to be tending toward a demise. Given the vigor of the 1950s, why the crisis and the chaos of the 1960s and the seemingly gloomy prospects for the 1970s?

For all the vigor of the 1950s, there were plenty of signs of weakness for those who cared to look at them. American Catholicism was defensive in both its organization and its mentality in the 1950s. There had been a great debate in nineteenth-century Catholicism between the Americanizers and the "anti-Americanizers," that is to say between those who felt that the Church could adopt an open and trusting posture toward the rest of society and those who argued that the faith of the immigrants had to be defended against the insidious attacks of that society. Even though the Americanizers won the arguments in theory, they lost the battle in practice. Even as recently as the nineteen twenties, there was still a substantial body of Catholic opinion that felt that millions of immigrants had been lost to the faith because the Church had not been vigilant enough to guard and protect them. It is possible now to say with considerable confidence that leakage from the Catholic Church has been relatively minor and that the immigrant experience seems to have enhanced the religious practice, if not the faith, of most Catholic groups in the population. Nevertheless, vigorous efforts were maintained in the nineteenth and the twentieth centuries to protect the immigrant faith. As far as was possible, a whole separate Catholic subculture was elaborated, running quite literally from the cradle to the grave and including Catholic schools, Catholic professional associations, Catholic social organizations, Catholic charities, Catholic insurance companies, and Catholic cemeteries. The strength of such institutions was reinforced by the fact that many immigrant groups' defense of the faith was taken to be the same as the defense of the culture of the mother country. If Catholic immigrants from Germany or Poland, for example, were to remain good Catholics, then it was necessary that they be good Germans or Poles. Since the immigrants clustered together with their fellows in any event, and since the Church was a pillar around which the immigrant groups could rally, the Church could count on strong social forces supporting the existence of a separate and distinct Catholic subculture.

Nor was there any doubt in the nineteenth century about the hostility of many groups in the American population. In the 1950s the memory of Al Smith's defeat still rankled in the breasts of many older Catholics, even though from its historical perspective, what was important about the Smith campaign was that he did so well despite his Catholicism. Anti-Catholic bigotry had not vanished in the 1950s, nor has it vanished even today. Indeed anti-Catholic feeling among American Jews seems to be increasing. Nevertheless, the violent hostility of the nativist American Protective Association and the Ku Klux Klan were things of the past. The 1960 campaign demonstrated that a Catholic could be elected President of the United States, if only by 110,000 votes, having lost perhaps five million votes because of his religion. But despite the fact that bigotry still existed in the 1950s, it was clear enough that the immigrant was going to keep the faith and that his children and grandchildren were, if anything, even more committed to the faith than he. Nevertheless, the defensive and protectionist structure of American Catholicism had not changed substantially. It was still being argued that Catholics should attend Catholic schools in order that their faith might be protected, although impressionistic evidence, soon to be followed by statistical data, indicated that very few Catholics did defect from their faith in the environment of non-Catholic schools. It was possible in the 1950s for a Catholic to attend the University of Chicago (as it had not been in the 1940s). But clergy and laity alike were still afraid of the pernicious influence of that university; the organizational structure of American Catholicism was still infected by the fear of the hostile non-Catholic environment, even though it was becoming increasingly obvious that this fear had become groundless.

The Catholicism of the 1950s assumed that it could count on the loyalty of the immigrant, since his faith was being attacked on all sides. When one had decided not to yield to the attack, one then forged tight bonds of unity with those who shared similar convictions. The loyalty of Catholic immigrants to their parishes was fierce and unquestioning. In well-to-do neighborhoods of the Southwest Side of Chicago in the 1950s, young people, when asked where they were from, would not name a street or neighborhood, but rather a parish. Their loyalty to the parish was rooted in the fact that the parish and its religion were an integral part of their own identity system. The immigrant may have been despised by the larger society, but at least in his parish church he had some sense of dignity and worth.

But while this loyalty was still quite evident in the 1950s, the basis for it was deteriorating. By the end of the decade, at least half the adult population was no longer of immigrants or even the children of immigrants (and only 10 per cent were immigrants). Catholics under forty were making as much money and were as well educated as anyone else in the population. Catholicism was still an important means of self-identification for most Americans. Nevertheless, the authority structure of the American Church was still rigid and autocratic, not to say authoritarian. Most bishops and pastors stood rather little on ceremony and could be quite democratic in their relationships, but when it came to decision making, they made the decisions and others carried them out. Catholicism had not changed since the Council of Trent and was not likely to. No matter that the authoritarian structure of the Council of Trent was designed for an authoritarian Renaissance society in which most Catholics were simple and uneducated. No matter that the American Church was now part of a democratic society with many of its members well educated. Some things were never going to change, and the authority structure was one of them.

But this confidence was risky. The children of immigrants were educated members of the upper middle class. Catholicism was now becoming fully accepted as a junior partner in the American experiment. Such changes called into question the basic assumptions of the authority structure. But the structure itself was taken as a "given" and was unlikely to change or even be capable of change.

Those in leadership positions had been chosen largely for reasons that were called "administrative." They had displayed abilities in doing the kinds of things that their predecessors in office had thought were required for the smooth functioning of the ecclesiastical structure. They were not, for the most part, scholars. Their important frame of reference was not the larger American society, which was increasingly affecting American Catholics, but the Roman Curia and its local representative, the apostolic delegate. While there were competent and able men among them—and an occasional genius—most of them were chosen because in the eyes of their ecclesiastical protectors, and of the apostolic delegate, they were "safe men," that is to say, men who could be counted on to resist the forces of change at all costs. Not only, then, was the authority structure resistant to change, but those who occupied the critical positions in the structure had been, for the most part, chosen precisely because they could be counted on to slow down change as much as possible on the rare occasions that it did seem to threaten. No one had bothered to ask, of course, what would happen to this kind of man when someone who sat at the very top of the authority pyramid should playfully start a fantastic process of change. If only that fat old gentleman hadn't opened his damn' window.

The Catholicism of the 1950s was ill-equipped to deal with ideas, as the various monographs of the Commission on Intellectual and Cultural Affairs, under the direction of the Reverend William Rooney, ably documented. There was little in the way of a climate of "respect for learning" in the American Church. Its leadership was still composed of the sons and daughters of the working class. Its orientation was practical and pragmatic. Achievement in American society and protection of the faith were the critical goals. Scholarship and intellectualism, if not viewed with suspicion, were at least thought to be superfluous. There was, of course, a great deal of anti-intellectualism in the rest of American Society, and Catholics were certainly not above sharing it. The tiny minority of authentic intellectuals, men such as Joseph Fichter, John Courtney Murray, Gustaf Weigel, Godfrey Diekman, were viewed with great suspicion. Murray was forbidden to write on the subject of the relationship between church and state, and "disinvited" to attend the first session of the Vatican Council. (Cardinal Spellman, however, succeeded in having him come to the second session, and Murray became one of the giant figures of the Council.) Several of these men were even forbidden to lecture at the Catholic University of America in the early 1960s.

However, as the ongoing research on Catholic intellectualism at the National Opinion Research Center has indicated, the new generation of American Catholics was growing up with serious intellectual concerns. The studies of Knap and his colleagues, as interpreted by Monsignor Ellis, described a very different kind of younger generation of Catholics from those described under the initial direction of James Allan Davis of the National Opinion Research Center. My colleagues and I are inclined to believe that the year 1957 marked the turning point as far as intellectual careers was concerned. Even though there are some Catholic liberals today who would still argue that the Catholic population of the United States is anti-intellectual, our research at NORC shows that the population under forty is at least as favorably disposed toward intellectualism as the rest of Americans. But the leadership of the Church was unaware of the change (and to some extent still is unaware of it) and had no notion of how important ideas would become in the 1960s. Furthermore, the ecclesiastical scholars and historians, theologians, sociologists, and psychologists who would have been indispensable in coping with the forces of change once they were let loose, simply did not exist in the 1950s. There were very few who thought it worth while to train such scholars.

One begins to see the potentially explosive nature of the situation —a population undergoing rapid social and economic change becoming more and more concerned with the things of the intellect and with personal freedom, and the structure viewing itself as unchangeable, showing no concern with the democratic process or with ideas, and taking as its permanent world view a situation in which it was necessary to defend the faith of an unlettered group of immigrants who were threatened by a hostile society.

Finally, the structures of American Catholicism had a fixed model of who was the ideal Catholic, and were quite unprepared for a new "breed" of Catholic laity who seriously questioned the model. The "good Catholic" was an essentialist. He had little sense of history and much sense of structure. He was concerned with defending and protecting, but not with relating. It would of course be helpful if he could understand what a dogma meant. But it was far more important that he be able to repeat the dogma accurately. It was helpful if he understood the reasons for what he was doing, but in case of doubt, it was far more important that he do what he was told than that he understand why. He didn't talk much about sex and hopefully didn't think too much about it either, even when he was busy procreating a large family.

But in the 1950s, the advance guard of the new breed was beginning to appear. Young peoples' philosophical orientations were existentialist. They were more concerned about Sartre, Kafka, Kierkegaard, and Camus than they were about Aquinas, Suárez, Bellarmine, and Aristotle, and if the truth be told, far more concerned about Sigmund Freud than they were about the Fathers of the First Vatican Council. Sex was, in their viewpoint, meant to be enjoyed, and vital and dynamic human relationships were far more important than obsolescent structures. Honesty and integrity were more important than respect and docility. Beliefs that were relevant for life were far more important than propositions that accurately reproduced credal formularies of the past.

The new breed was just that—a new breed which the men of the 1950s did not expect and with which they were quite incapable of coping.

Organizationally, then, the church of the 1950s was prospering. It represented the finest flourishing of immigrant Catholicism, and in some ways was extraordinarily impressive. The immigrants and their children had built the most extensive and elaborate religious institutional structure in the world. It was John Courtney Murray who remarked, "Good, very good indeed, but not good enough."

And it was not good enough precisely because it was too rigid to change, too rigid even to be aware that the forces of change were swirling about it and that despite its prosperity and apparent success, it was in for very heavy weather indeed.

When the Catholicism of the 1950s is viewed in retrospect, it becomes fairly clear that most of the problems that the Church faced at the end of the 1960s would have existed even if there had been no Second Vatican Council. The Council certainly accelerated the forces of change. It gave legitimacy and a sense of urgency to those Catholics who were growing impatient with what they thought was the narrow, rigid, defensive, inflexible structure of the working-class-immigrant authoritarian Church. The Council made it quite clear that the Church was capable of dramatic change, and that discussion, dialogue, and controversy were by no means impossible within the Catholic framework. The daily press accounts of the vigorous debates of the Vatican Council made American Catholics well aware that things could change in the Church, even things that had been thought unchangeable. The weak link in the armor had been found, for once a single apparently immutable structure is questioned, then everything else is able to be questioned. The questions would have been asked anyhow, but the Vatican Council caused them to be asked earlier and with greater consistency. Furthermore, the Council also brought to the attention of the American public the ideas of some of the theologians of Europe, ideas that the increasingly restless elite groups of the Catholic population found much to their liking. That triumphal tour of the young Swiss theologian Huns Küng through the United States during the Council was a major turning point. When Küng spoke of the freedom and honesty in the Church, he did so in terms that the new breed of American Catholics thought corresponded rather precisely to their own inarticulate longings. Similarly the visit of Augustin Cardinal Bea to Harvard University to speak of ecumenism gave considerable comfort to those Catholics who thought it was time for the Counter Reformation to come to an end.

The immigrant Church was in its sunset glory in the 1950s. There would have been trouble in the 1960s in any case, but the end of the immigrant age, signaled by the inauguration of John Kennedy, happened to correspond with the end of the Counter Reformation signaled by Augustin Bea on the stage of Sander's Theatre at Harvard University.

The combination of these two dramatic changes in Roman Catholicism meant trouble to an institutional structure that was not predisposed to change.

The lid was about to blow off.

THE 1960s

In the last section, I suggested that the present problems of American Catholicism can be viewed as a result of a rapid change in the culture of American Catholics, without any corresponding change in the structure of the Church. This change in the culture of Catholics was in its turn rooted in the change of the structure of American society. Catholics became full-fledged members of the American polity, economy, and prestige structure. As they did, the values of loyalty and defensiveness became less important. Values of openness, democracy, and dialogue became more important. But the structure of the Counter Reformation immigrant Church could not cope with these values. Nor would the new breed of young clerics and lay persons who were arguing such values, create new structures of their own.

In this section I intend to discuss how four of the structural patterns of the American Church were affected by the surge of new ideas in the late fifties and early sixties. The inadequate response of the structures to the new values produced a paradox. Those who had, in the name of the new values, attacked the old structure found themselves without any structure. The old institutions were substantially weakened, but the new values have not yet generated new patterns of relationships, with the result that in many instances the forces of change in American Catholicism left themselves with practically no structural base and were quite unable to create one. To put the matter in non-sociological terms, they threw out the baby with the bath and now can find neither the baby nor the bathtub.

Perhaps a classic example of this process is the peculiar situation with regard to Catholic education. Most of the leaders of change in the American Church are the product of Catholic schools. Many of them are employed by Catholic schools. Nevertheless, they have launched a violent attack on Catholic education, with only the vaguest and most romantic ideas of what might replace it. They now find themselves losing the institutional base that Catholic education provided, and have discovered that if structure without culture is ossified, then culture without structure is chaotic. As we shall note later on, it is precisely the ones who are most in the vanguard of the forces of change who have the least tolerance for ambiguity and chaos. Having set out, then, to destroy the structural system, they all too frequently end up destroying themselves.

In 1960, Catholic education could look back on what had been the most impressive two decades in its history. Its enrollment had climbed steadily, and it was undergoing dramatic internal reform; new schools

—primary, secondary, and higher—were being opened at a rapid clip; its graduates were beginning to seriously pursue academic careers; and attendance at the Catholic school correlated positively with social class, showing that as Catholics moved up the economic and social ladder they became more, rather than less, dedicated to their schools. Somewhere between two thirds and three quarters of the Catholic population in the country favored the continuation of Catholic education. About one half of the Catholics in the country of primary and secondary school age were in Catholic schools; two thirds of those whose parents desired any kind of religious education for their children were in such schools.

A decade later, enrollment is declining and schools are closing, and a moratorium has been declared on the construction of high schools and grammar schools. Catholic educators are asking themselves whether there is any future in Catholic education, and the fear that Catholic education must be "phased out" is openly expressed.

Such a change would be amazing enough in itself, but it is even more amazing when one ponders the fact that there is no evidence at all that the general Catholic population has changed its thinking on Catholic schools. The Ben Gaffin study of 1952, the NORC study of 1963, the Gallup study of 1965, the Louis Harris/Newsweek study of 1967, and the various diocesan surveys and censuses of 1969 show remarkable similarity in the proportions of Catholics in favor of parochial education. There has been, in effect, no change in the attitude of Catholics on the subject of Catholic schools. Furthermore, there is increased sympathy toward these schools in non-Catholic circles; with the apparent failure of the public school systems to cope with urban educational problems, there is an increased predisposition for public support of a variety of private school systems on the urban scene. In other words, Catholic schools are apparently undergoing a disaster at the same time that their image is improving in the world outside the Church.

The problem of Catholic education, then, seems to be one of internal morale. The whole elaborate structure was toppled by a handful of authors whose books were unencumbered by conclusive data or persuasive theory and were read by only a handful of the Catholic population. But they *were* read by the Catholic educators, whose confidence in what they were doing was apparently so weak that the slightest push could topple it. What the pushers did, of course, was to question the old defensive, protectionist, lower-middle-class, immigrant rationale of Catholic education. The educators themselves, for the most part, were well aware that this rationale was no longer adequate. But they were not capable of creating a new rationale or of modifying the structure of Catholic education in such a way as to suggest what a new rationale might be. The change in the culture had a devastating effect on the structure and did not produce any new positive values or a new structure. American Catholicism lacked flexibility to create new positive values. We shall have to return to this explanation repeatedly.

In almost any conversation between Catholic educators, a new conventional wisdom has emerged on the subject of Catholic education. One sets this wisdom down because it is an excellent illustration of the self-defeating complex in which American Catholicism is currently caught:

1.   The American Church cannot afford to meet the increasing costs of its educational system.

2.   Catholic schools are not accomplishing what they were designed to do, that is to say, producing more-devout and more-religious Catholics.

3.   Catholic schools are divisive, because they isolate their students from the rest of American society.

4.   Catholic schools are losing the support of most Catholic lay people.

5.   Catholic schools are not reaching most American Catholics.

6.   Catholic schools are not reaching those most in need of education—the poor.

7.   Catholic schools are needlessly duplicating the work of the home.

8.   What is being done in Catholic schools can be accomplished in

Sunday schools or released-time schools with considerably less expenditure of money and personnel.

9. Catholic schools are inferior to public schools academically.

10. Despite their claims to be Catholic, there is not an authentically charitable atmosphere inside Catholic schools.

11. Catholic colleges are losing money and cannot be expected to survive the financial crisis of the years ahead.

12. The alumni of Catholic colleges are so dissatisfied at what happened in their education that they are unlikely to want to send their children to the same schools they attended.

I am sure that most readers have heard this conventional wisdom many times. Perhaps so often that it is taken for granted that it is true. But I must assert that, in fact, the conventional wisdom is false. Indeed, every one of the propositions that I have listed is demonstrably false. This is not the time or the place to provide a comprehensive defense of Catholic education, even if I had the inclination to elaborate such a defense. But, nonetheless, one can assert:

1. No one knows whether Catholics are willing or able to bear the burden of increased expenses of their educational system. No one knows, because no one has really asked.

2. The graduates of Catholic schools are, according to most available measures, more religious than Catholics who did not go to Catholic schools.

3. No one has been able to find the slightest trace of evidence that Catholic schools have any divisive effect upon American society.

4. Every survey done in the past decade and a half demonstrates a high and consistent level of support for Catholic schools.

5. Catholic schools are reaching about two thirds of the available Catholic students, available, that is, in terms of their parents' interest in religious education of any sort.

6. Far more than any other private school system, and more effectively than most public school systems, Catholic schools in the inner city are reaching the black poor, at least those of the poor who have any disposition toward upper mobility, and are evidently popular with most blacks.

7. Catholic schools do not duplicate what goes on at home. On the contrary, the most notable effect is had when home and school independently reinforce one another.

8. There is no evidence of any sort that the various substitute forms of religious education have any impact at all.

9. The graduates of Catholic schools consistently do better in the national norms on standardized achievement tests, and Catholics who went to Catholic schools are more successful socially and economically and academically than Catholics who went to public schools, with all background variables held constant. They are also, interestingly enough, more liberal politically and socially.

10. Research by my colleague Donald Light demonstrates that Catholic high schools are making far more academic demands and their students are also more skillful in integrating into the school life those who are disadvantaged economically, socially, or humanly.

11. Catholic higher education is running in the black economically, at least as of a year and a half ago. In addition, the typical Catholic school is in better economic shape than a typical private non-Catholic college.

12. Even though the alumni of Catholic colleges are fully aware of the weaknesses of their educational experience, they are still more loyal to their schools and more likely to want to send their children there than is the typical American alumnus.

I am, of course, well aware that the data on which my assertions are based will have little or no effect on the conventional wisdom. But one must still ask why, in the face of such data, particularly when they are combined with a high and consistent level of popular support and increasingly favorable disposition in the non-Catholic world, has the morale of Catholic educators collapsed?

The schools suffer from the fact that they are large and obvious institutions, and like all educational institutions, easy targets for scapegoating. All the dissatisfaction with the rigid and inflexible institutional structure of the American Church can be taken out on the Catholic schools, even though the schools are probably more flexible than most American Catholic institutions. Those who are angry at the Pope, at Catholic sexual doctrine, at their bishops, at their religious superior, at their pastor, or at anybody else in sight, can blame their anger and frustration on Catholic education. Are there racists to be found in the Catholic population? Why didn't the schools eliminate them! Is there anti-intellectualism in certain elements of the Catholic population? That is the schools' fault. Are Catholics in favor of the war in Vietnam? Blame it on the schools. Is liturgical reform proceeding slowly? It is because Catholic schools weren't pushing such reform in the nineteen thirties and forties.[3] When any human institution has become so much ink blot, it is in serious danger. And the mere fact that statistical data seem to exonerate it of most of the serious charges made against it, is going to be quite irrelevant. Catholic schools are bad and must be phased out, or at least are going to be phased out even if not bad, and that is that. Please don't bother us with facts.

The schools also suffer from self-hatred, which is almost inevitable in later stages of the acculturation process of immigrant groups. The immigrant's grandson has finally broken out of the walls of the old neighborhood and now stands eager, but somewhat frightened, in the midst of the larger society. He looks back at what he has come from and feels ashamed of it. Boston College is not Harvard. Regis H.S. Prep is not Groton. St. Francis Grammar School is not the North Shore Country Day School. The Church's bishops are not scholars, its pastors not intellectuals; there is nothing in American Catholicism that is any good. The seeds of self-hatred were, of course, sown during the days of belligerent defensive Catholicism. The grandson of the immigrant has to be out of the ghetto for a while before he does not have to feel defensive about his origins and is freed from the necessity of validating himself in the eyes of the outside world by attacking that from which he came. But just as several centuries of the white assumption that blacks were inferior was hard on black self-confidence, so a century and a half of non-Catholic attack on Catholic schools prepared Catholic educators for believing the abso-

[3] See on this matter Mary Perkins Ryan, *Are Parochial Schools the Answer* (Holt, New York, 1964), the classic statement of the simplistic attack on Catholic education.

lute worst about themselves. In the present time of transition, many educators seem almost eager to believe the worst.

The collapse of morale in Catholic schools, then, can be attributed to the use of the schools as a scapegoat, and to the self-hatred of the later stages of the acculturation process. Neither of these factors was irresistible. Under certain sets of circumstances one could imagine that Catholic education would have responded to the crisis of the early sixties by taking two decisive steps:

1. A new rationale for Catholic education based in part on the challenges of the present moment and in part on the accomplishments the Catholic past could have been elaborated.

2. The internal structure of the schools could have been dramatically democratized; the schools could have taken the lead in the movements for change in the Church, instead of becoming their scapegoat.

But no new theories were elaborated, though heaven knows the raw material for such theories was present; and the democratization process in the schools was much too slow. The experience of the schools can be taken as paradigmatic of the other failures of American Catholicism in the 1960s. The Church failed to generate new positive values and new, open, and flexible structures.

Ecclesiastical authority is, if anything, in more trouble than Catholic schools, for while the schools still command the loyalty of the general population, consensus is being withdrawn from authority by the general population in certain areas such as sex, and by elite groups within the population on almost all subjects. The credibility and legitimacy of ecclesiastical authority is under direct attack. Some demonstrate open contempt for it. Many more simply ignore it. Perhaps 80 per cent of the Catholic population do not take seriously the Church's teachings on birth control. An increasingly substantial proportion do not believe its teaching on divorce. Most priests under forty-five no longer say the breviary. The hierarchy has lost complete control over liturgical reform. Parish priests, on their own initiative, are granting permission for people to be married after divorce and to continue to receive the sacraments. The mistakes and failings of leadership are ruthlessly criticized. Attempts to declare certain issues "closed" are ignored. Threats of punishment are ridiculed, and warnings of danger are laughed at. As hard as it may be for ecclesiastical leadership to admit it, there is every reason to think that the leadership is rapidly becoming irrelevant in the American Church. It still controls funds, but one is forced to wonder how long there will even be funds for it to control.

Why has the ecclesiastical authority lost credibility so completely and so quickly? I would like to advance as a hypothesis what I call the "Meat on Friday" theory. Once change is introduced in something that is of high symbolic importance, the whole symbol system is put in serious jeopardy. Theoretically, the prohibition against meat on Friday was an unimportant part of Catholic practice. It took on high symbolic importance in the American environment, because it distinguished Catholics from Protestants. If one admits that such an important symbol can be changed, then all other important symbols are called in to question, and the whole tight network is seriously threatened. I am certainly not suggesting that the abolition of Friday abstinence has *caused* the crisis in authority in the American Church. What I am arguing, rather, is that once one begins to fiddle with the symbol system, the whole system is in jeopardy unless a new and persuasive symbol system can be elaborated. Authority is in trouble in the American Church precisely because it cannot understand the need to modify its relationship to the rest of the Church and to elaborate a new symbol system to explain its position. On the contrary, in the last half of the decade of the sixties it seemed, rather, to do just the opposite. It insisted that nothing much had changed, and that nothing more was going to change. In the 1950s such statements would have been accepted, but too much happened between 1959 and 1965 for these statements to continue to command credibility. Every new attempt on the part of the ecclesiastical leadership to stop the tide of change simply reduces its effectiveness the more. Leadership still has the power to command, or thinks it has, but it no longer has the power to obtain consensus. Authority without the power to obtain consensus is empty authority.

The clergy is also in serious trouble, and by clergy we use the word in the broad sense, including priests, nuns, and brothers. As we pointed out in the previous subsection (see Table 1, p. 164), there has been a drastic decline both in vocations and in the ratio of clergy to the population. In addition to quantitative loss, the clergy have also lost assurance of their role and function. They are no longer sure of who they are and what they should be doing. A substantial number have left the priesthood and the religious life and others seem to be caught in a malaise of indecision and doubt. Various associations of priests and religious have appeared around the country, and national federations have been established. While these groups have somewhat increased the power of the clergy, they have not been successful in providing a new rationale or direction for the clerical and religious life. In addition, it seems to be precisely those religious communities that most thoroughly modernize themselves that suffer the greatest loss in personnel, for reasons we will discuss later. Finally, the evaporation of vocations appears even worse when one considers that it is precisely among the upper-middle-class, well-educated segments of the population that it is most difficult to recruit young men and women for the clergy. When later immigrant groups reach that stage of acculturation, one can expect vocations to dry up almost completely. In the meantime, the American Church will be faced with a situation in which an increasing proportion of clergy will come from lower social-class backgrounds than their congregations.

The decline of the clergy is even more surprising when one remembers that it did not take a whole decade, but has occurred mostly since 1965. The enthusiasm and excitement of the Vatican Council produced great expectations of how fast the Church would change. But the collapse of these expectations, coupled with the increasing uncertainty of the roles and functions of the cleric, has created a near-panic among the younger clergy and religious. They are disillusioned about renewal; they do not believe their leaders; they lack a sense of participation in decision making; they do not know what to do with the new freedom they have found; and they are very much afraid of the future.

The old clerical culture was doomed, though in the 1950s one would not have thought that it would collapse so quickly. The old value system, which stressed the role of the priest as the leader and protector of a defensive immigrant population, no longer has much validity. It was easy to demolish it, just as it was easy to demolish the old justification for a Catholic school system or for autocratic authority. But to demolish was one thing, and to create new values and the structure for these new values was something quite different. In the 1960s, American Catholicism went through a period of extremely rapid demolition, with very little in the way of new construction.

Finally, the established behavior patterns of sexuality of American Catholics have dramatically changed. As we have previously suggested, this change was well under way even in the 1950s. What actually happened in the 1960s is that the groups that were most likely to adhere to the old norms—principally well-educated Irish Catholics—seem to have abandoned the norms completely. There were clergy in the 1950s who expressed private doubts about Catholic birth-control teaching. But the principal difference between the fifties and the sixties is that the younger clergy (those under forty) are not only willing to express these doubts publicly but to act upon them in the confessional. If the birth-control theory can be questioned, then there seems to be no reason—at least in the minds of many—why the Church's position on divorce and, indeed, premarital and extramarital sexuality, and even homosexuality, can also be called into question. Furthermore, such related doctrines as the desirability of a large family and the restriction of the woman to the role of wife and mother, are also under heavy attack. Ecclesiastical celibacy has become a scapegoat for the failure of the Church to understand the problems in its rigid birth-control positions, and a change in obligatory celibacy is advocated by many clergy and laity as a symbol of a difference between the "old Church" and the "new Church." There is some evidence to indicate that for most priests celibacy is not nearly as important as other issues, but it has tremendous symbolic value precisely, because the whole context of the Catholic stand on sexuality is now being seriously questioned.

Sex is certainly the most corrosive issue facing Roman Catholicism at the present time, an issue that, for the Catholic Church, is something analogous to what the Vietnam war is for the American republic. It is, as we shall see, the only subject on which the mass of the population is as disaffected as the elites. The issue is not merely birth control or celibacy. These are indeed painful and powerful issues for many Catholics, but the issue is a wider one: the credibility of the Church's response to the Freudian revolution.

Once again, however, we see the same forces at work: an old value system collapsed; old structures were called into question; new positive values did not replace the old ones, nor have new structures been elaborated. The result is chaos and confusion. Those who attack the old values are almost as confused as everyone else, if not more so. Thus, many of the clergy who were outspoken in their attack on the Church's birth-control teaching now find themselves puzzled as to how to cope with their own sexuality, either in marriage or in celibacy, a sexuality that, in the 1950s, they would have been afraid even to discuss. Now it often seems they are quite incapable of discussing anything else.

The rigid structure of the Church prevented questions about the values behind Catholic schools, Catholic sexuality, the functions of authority, and the role of the clergy from arising before 1960, but when they finally did come out into the open, as a result of the Vatican Council, they came out with explosive force. The leadership of the Church was unable to modify its structures in response to the questions raised, and neither the leaders nor the questioners have been able to elaborate new value systems to take the place of the old.

If one wanted to summarize in a single sentence the story of American Catholicism in the 1960s, one could say that the old has been destroyed but the new has not been built.

II

Every collectivity has certain agents or institutions that are responsible for anticipating and preparing for change. Whether the agent is called a market researcher, a prophet, a magician, or a futurologist, his job is critical. He is the one who must remind the rest of the collectivity that the present situation is not necessarily permanent, much less eternal. In the modern world, most large corporate groups have two such institutions, which are, at least part of the time, responsible for anticipating and preparing for change: administrators and intellectuals. The former are supposed to spot the indicators of change in their daily exercise of responsibility, and modify their behavior to adjust to that change. The latter, operating on a more speculative basis, are supposed to ask how changing social and technical reality can be expected to influence the given collectivity, and what long-range response to such influence is in order. I suggested in the preceding pages that American Catholicism wasn't able to modify either its values or its structures sufficiently to be able to respond to the explosion occasioned by the Vatican Council. The administrators were not able to generate enough new ideas. The clergy, who share in part the role of both the administrator and the scholar, being low-level administrators and popular theorizers, were unable to compensate for the failures of the hierarchy and the intellectual community. I am contending, therefore, that American Catholicism failed to respond to the challenge in the 1960s because neither the hierarchy nor the clergy nor the intellectuals were able to respond.

I must note in passing that a fourth institution, the laity, is deliberately excluded from my consideration because the masses of the laity are not organized yet in any way that would give them leverage on what happens in the institutional Church. Some clergymen would say that the laity simply are not interested, and some laity will say that the clergy have not permitted them to be interested. But in ei-

ther case, or any combination of the two cases, the laity in the 1960s
have not been an institution to which one could have reasonably
looked for an adequate response to the challenges that the Church
faced.

I should also note in passing that I will have to say some unpleasant things about hierarchy, clergy, and intellectuals. The hierarchy
are used to being criticized. The clergy, somewhat less so; and the
intellectuals have assumed that they are immune to criticism. There
is something in this section, as Mort Sahl has remarked in another
context, to offend just about everyone.

I do not think that the failure of the leadership of the Church to
respond to the crisis of the 1960s can be attributed to malice, or
even specifically to the fear of the loss of power. Although no man
willingly gives up power, the major problem is the hierarchy's failure
to adequately assess the situation. For a number of different reasons,
ecclesiastical leadership has thought that the pace of change has been
too fast, whereas in fact their response to the pace of change has
been too slow. The forces that were pent up during the 1950s and
released by the Vatican Council, were powerful and highly dynamic.
Ecclesiastical leadership could have chosen, as Pope John did, to
ride the crest of these forces and take credit for them. Or it could
have chosen to become frightened by the power and the intensity
of the forces, and to try to slow them down to what seemed like
manageable speed. In the former set of circumstances, one would
make an act of faith in the basic thrust of the modern human community and in the vigorous demands of the elite segments of the
Catholic population. In the latter course of action, one would be
suspicious and fearful of the modern world and afraid that the pride
of those demanding change within the Church would lead them
away from sound doctrine and from faith itself. Those who advocated the second course of action were characterized by Pope John
as the Prophets of Doom. One need only pick up a weekly Catholic
newspaper to discover that the Prophets of Doom are currently in
the ascendancy.

It was, I think, possible at the beginning of Pope Paul's reign, to see clearly the goals he established for himself:

1. A smooth transition from the pre-Vatican to the post-Vatican Church, with as little strife and conflict as possible;
2. A defense of the credibility and effective authority of the Papacy;
3. A gradual reform and modernization of the Roman Curia;
4. A fruitful dialogue with the modern world that would not compromise traditional Catholic beliefs;
5. The maintenance of the credibility of Catholic sexual teaching;
6. A careful construction of new and effective institutions of authority and administration in the Church.

I do not think it an exaggeration to say at this time that none of these goals have been achieved. The Church is torn by conflict and dissension. The sexual teaching of the Church is no longer respected by a large part of its membership. Dialogue with Protestants, not to say the secular world, goes very slowly. The prestige of the Papacy is at a very low ebb. The Roman Curia has not been effectively reformed, and new institutions of administration perform poorly, if at all.

One can, of course, engage in reporting the backstairs gossip about the politics of the Roman Curia and how the decisions that have created this situation were made. But, in fact, whatever the politics were, it does seem clear that the Pope decided that the pace of change was too rapid, that he had to exercise a restraining influence. This restraining influence has not been successful. In retrospect, one cannot avoid the conclusion that the Pope would have been much better advised to imitate his predecessor and take vigorous and dramatic command of the direction of change.

When those in the position of leadership attempt to brake social forces that are too powerful to be restrained, they run the risk of losing control completely.

The same phenomena seem to have occurred in the American

Church. The classic example of this is the matter of liturgical reform. Once the Vatican Council's declaration on liturgy gave ideological approval to the idea of an active and humanly relevant liturgy, the pressure for dramatic modification and experimentation in liturgy became very great. The American hierarchy, in fact, took a far more enlightened stand than did most of the other hierarchies in the world on liturgical change, and put more pressure on the Vatican for permission to experiment than did most other hierarchies. But the changes that were authorized came more slowly than those who were demanding change were willing to tolerate. Increasingly, then, the liturgical reformers—and this includes a very large segment of the clergy—took innovation into their own hands. Approval of change has been perhaps eighteen months behind the fact of change. Under such circumstances, the credibility of those to whom one is supposed to look for approval is badly impaired.

When it became clear to the bishops of the country that liturgical innovation was going on completely out of their control, they responded in two ways. Some of them "withdrew from the field." That is to say, they pretended that the liturgy issue did not exist, and made it quite clear that they simply did not want to hear of the unauthorized experiments that were taking place. The other response was to insist that now was the time to "put the lid on." The advocates of this strategy refused to seek permission for further experimentation and innovation, and did their best to restrain the unauthorized experimentation that was going on. Both responses ignored one important fact: the vigor with which liturgical reform was being pushed by the clergy and the laity was a sign that such reform responded to very powerful and important religious needs.

The pattern of challenge and response in the liturgical area is paradigmatic for the crisis in the 1960s. Vigorous demands were responded to slowly. Those who made the demands acted on their own. Faced with the chaos and confusion created by this initiative, leadership attempted to terminate the initiative. Those who had taken the initiative continued on their own, and communication between them and leadership ended. To respond too slowly means trouble. To attempt to "put the lid on" means disaster. Yet Church leadership in the United States—and in most of the Church, too, for that matter—committed both these mistakes during the 1960s.

The critical question is why they misread the situation. Why were they afraid of responding quickly to the fluid situation created by the Council, and why did they think they could "put the lid on"? Many of them seem to have persuaded themselves that the majority of the laity were "scandalized" by the sort of changes that were occurring, although, in fact, every attempt that has been made to gather systematic data on the subject shows that between three fourth and seven eighth of the Catholic population were in sympathy with most of the changes taking place in the Church. We are then forced to ask another question: why did the leadership of the Church think that the "faithful are being scandalized," when in fact this was not happening?

It is fashionable in some Catholic circles to suggest that bishops are stupid or malicious or incompetent, but this is hardly an adequate explanation. The hierarchy, one presumes, like every other human group, does include some malice and some stupidity and some incompetence. But it also has intelligent, competent, generous, and open-minded men. And in Cardinal Dearden it has one of the most able presidents of any hierarchy in the world. The problem is not so much in individuals, but in a system that may have been adequate in the 1940s and even the 1950s, but is less than adequate to the challenges it had to face in the 1960s. American bishops were chosen, as we remarked earlier, on a highly personal basis. Men were made bishops, on the judgment of the apostolic delegate or some of the powerful "kingmakers" in the American hierarchy, that they were suitable and "safe" men. Some very able and effective leaders were so chosen. But the choices of the various delegates and of the "kingmakers" were inevitably subjective, and many men found themselves in the hierarchy because they had been diligent in "playing the game" of cultivating the powerful figures and not because they had any real ability as leaders of other human beings. Renaissance court politics— and in some instances the power struggles of the American Church are just that—may be excellent training for a Renaissance court, but such activity does not necessarily qualify one to respond to a highly dynamic situation created by the release of pent-up social forces. While there are some scholars among the bishops, there is not nearly enough intelligence. While there are some secure and visionary human beings, there are also too many who are both frightened and timid. While there are some who are utterly fearless, there are too many who are terribly worried about their own "careers." And for some, the only important reference group is composed of other bishops and the Roman Curia. While there are some who are young in years, and some more who are young in ideas, there are many who are old in both ideas and years. While there are a few who are able to communicate very effectively beyond the limits of bishops' meetings, there are many, many more who not only lack all skills at communication, but do not even understand that they have a communication problem. While there are some who are very able at responding to fluid and changing situations, there are many more who fall back on an arbitrary exercise of power when faced with a situation the response to which is not provided for in the Code of Canon Law. While there are some who have surrounded themselves with excellent staffs and know how to work with such staffs, there are many more who have surrounded themselves with incompetent sycophants and could not use good staff people even if they were able to recognize them when they saw them.

Another way of saying the same thing is to point out that the ecclesiastical leadership is, to a very considerable extent, well suited to the lower-middle and working class, immigrant, static Church that existed before the end of the Second World War. The only trouble is that that Church doesn't exist any more, and will never exist again.

The situation is all the more astonishing when one stops to consider that in the nineteenth century, the American Church produced some extraordinary leaders—men whose ideas and vision anticipated the Vatican Council by more than a century, in some instances. John Carroll, the first bishop of the United States, vigorously advocated the vernacular liturgy because, as he said, the people could not understand Latin. John England, the first Bishop of Charleston, in 1825 turned over the government of his diocese to an elected board of clergy and laity—ten laity and five clergy. John Ireland, the great curmudgeon of St. Paul, practiced ecumenism long before the word was invented. His sometime friend and sometime foe, John Lancaster Spalding, the tragic Bishop of Peoria, preached about the importance of science, culture, and rights for women in language that would be as modern and striking today as it was when he first used it, in the last quarter of the past century. John Keane, the first rector of the Catholic University of America, preached in the Harvard Divinity School chapel seven decades before Cardinal Bea.

Those who seek for an explanation of the change in the quality of the American hierarchy since those days usually cite four factors:

1. The creation of the North American College in Rome, where future leaders of the Church would be socialized into acceptable curial mentality;

2. The appointment of an apostolic delegate who could carefully supervise what went on in the American Church and restrain the freewheeling behavior of liberals such as Keane, Spalding, and Ireland;

3. The shudder of reaction that went through the whole Church at the time of the Modernism controversy at the beginning of the present century;

4. The humiliation of the intellectual leaders of the American hierarchy with the condemnation of the so-called "Americanist" heresy —a heresy that, if it existed at all, existed not in America but in a few books by French authors.

To these explanations I would add two more:

1. Modern methods of transportation and communication give the Roman Curia far more effective control over what happens everywhere in the world than it had a half century ago.

2. The apostolic delegates who have been sent to the United States tend to be very conservative, and tend to have chosen very conservative men for critical positions in the American Church. The Canadian

hierarchy, which seems to be better able to cope with the present crisis than the American hierarchy, was chosen by men who, if they were not exactly liberal, were somewhat more progressive than the various apostolic delegates to the United States.

But, for whatever reasons, the fact remains that the American hierarchy was not able to respond, despite some excellent leadership and the presence of many competent and dedicated men. The hierarchy was not flexible enough or imaginative enough to cope with the crisis of the 1960s. Indeed, one must say many do not even seem to have understood that there is a crisis.

It is fashionable to say critical things about the hierarchy. It is unfashionable, however, to say critical things about the so-called Catholic intelligentsia. But I would contend that their failure has been at least as grievous as has the failure of the hierarchy. I presume an intelligentsia has two functions: it criticizes the old, and it hypothesizes about the new. The American Catholic intelligentsia, as far as one exists at all, has been effective in criticizing the old, but has resolutely refused to prophesy about the new. It has been unable to do so, because its rejection of the old is so categoric and so total that it does not permit itself to have any hopes for the new to emerge. We need only read through the two principle organs of the so-called Catholic intelligentsia of the United States—the *National Catholic Reporter* and *Commonweal*—to discover that they are waspish, strident, shrill, and negative. There is precious little vision of hope in either of them. Given the immense influence that these journals have on the elite groups within the American Church, their failure to elaborate a vision toward which one might strive, and to discover developments that seem to be pointing in the direction of such a vision, must be considered as a major failure.

Intellectuals would reply that their function is to criticize and not to create, that the whole structure is so rotten that it must be torn down completely so that one can start anew, and finally, that if they see no hope it may well be because there is no hope to be seen.

One may only compare their efforts to those of their European counterparts to determine the magnitude of the failure of the American Catholic intelligentsia. The European theological journal *Concilium*, for example, shows how vigorous, hopeful, and enthusiastic European scholarship is in the midst of an ecclesiastical situation that, if anything, is worse than that in the United States. The positive, constructive, and hopeful tone of *Concilium*, in contrast to the negative, destructive, and pessimistic tone of American Catholic intelligentsia, is even more astonishing when one stops to consider that we Americans are supposed to be a hopeful and optimistic people.

How can one explain this failure of Catholic intelligentsia in the United States? One must first of all note that most of those who shape the thinking and opinions of the Catholic elites are not scholars in the sense that the various editors and writers of *Concilium* are. American Catholicism in the 1950s did not produce many scholars. It did not respect the few that it did produce. The European scholarly heroes who visit us and are acclaimed are not really understood. My colleague Karl Rahner, for example, is quoted out of context with the same dogmatic authoritarianism with which St. Thomas Aquinas was quoted not too many years ago. And my colleague Hans Küng runs the risk of having a paragraph lifted out of context from his writings and turned into the basis for an elaborate apostolic program. These men and their counterparts in Europe are horrified and puzzled when such things happen. It is very difficult to convey to them the fact that even though scholarship now is very popular in the American Church, it is not understood, nor appreciated for what it is.

In the absence of scholars, then, the function of the intelligentsia is usurped totally by a group that is by rights only part of the intelligentsia—the journalists. It is no exaggeration to say that a handful of Catholic journalists, some of them on Catholic magazines and newspapers, and others working in the secular media, have personally, and through their contacts in the secular media, become the intellectual leaders of the American Church. While many of them are good and admirable men, it is not unfair to say that they are not qualified for the task. Some of them are graduate-school dropouts, many of them ex-seminarians, and most of them quite angry at the ecclesiastical institution. Their self-hatred is strong, their envy of the Protestant and Jewish intellectual and journalistic establishment is powerful, and their desire to be part of the avant-garde at times almost embarrassing. With little qualification and less modesty, they presume to sit in judgment, in, for example, the book-review section of the New York *Times*, on some of the great European scholars, one of whom described a popular American journalist-intellectual as a theologically illiterate dilettante.

But these men have immense influence because of the virtual monopoly they enjoy as opinion makers, and because many of the elites are willing to take them with absolute seriousness, as purveyors of total truth—just as Aquinas was, not so many years ago.

The journalist-intellectuals tend to be angry, bitter, pessimistic, superficial men who are marvelously good at tearing down and quite uninterested in building up. Through careful manipulation of book reviews, news stories, feature articles, and letters columns, they systematically suppress any information about positive or constructive developments in the American Church. One reads their journals in vain to find, for example, any sign of the experimentation that is obvious in the grass roots of the American Church and that is so impressive to European visitors. The only news, apparently, that is fit to print, is bad news.

In addition, the journalist-intellectuals, through their control of book reviews in both their own and secular journals, are able to systematically bar from public notice many writers whose claim of scholarship would be unquestioned. Thus Eugene Kennedy, whose ideas on religion and sexuality are extraordinarily creative and whose books are widely read, has been almost completely ignored by the influential Catholic journals. And other writers, such as Victor Ferkis, whose ideas do not fit the party line of liberal intellectuals, are given scant notice.

I am not contending that the journalist-intellectuals are engaged in a conspiracy. Their position is so unique and so powerful that they do not need to conspire. They are almost immune to criticism and can easily write off those who dare to criticize, as being conservative or ambitious for admission to the hierarchy. They can play loose with facts and sometimes engage in behavior whose ethics are highly questionable. When the *Education of Catholic Americans* first appeared in 1965, an editorial writer in *Commonweal* dismissed it as an attempt to whitewash Catholic schools. At the same time, a story in the New York *Times* systematically selected all unfavorable information about Catholic schools for an article that excluded anything that might be favorable about such schools. The religion editor of the *Times* later apologized to me, but the apology never seemed to find its way into print. Finally, the editor of the *National Catholic Reporter* wrote an ambiguous editorial that he later admitted was based on a very hasty reading of the book and his assumptions about what my "position" really was. Note that the book on the one hand was criticized for whitewashing the Catholic schools, and on the other hand was used as a means of criticizing the schools.

In one instance, a prominent journal assigned to a reviewer a book whose author was supposed to have had an affair with the wife of the reviewer. Even though this fact was called to the attention of the editor of the magazine, the review still appeared. Another journalist-intellectual submitted an article to a journal that was a particularly nasty, personal assault on the same hapless author, without bothering to state that he was a close friend of the allegedly aggrieved husband. The editor of this journal—which is not part of the "establishment" of the intellectual-journalist—removed the paragraph in question.

The journalist-intellectuals are, in their own way, pathetic men. They have lived off the institutional Church for much of their lives; and those who no longer do so have made it to where they are, for the most part, because of the national position that they were able to obtain through commenting on the Church. They have participated eagerly in the destruction of old structures and values, and are horrified that now their institutional base is eroding. They lament the fact that the hierarchy does not take them seriously, and cannot face the fact that many of the clergy and laity take them far too seriously. They have been able to play the role of scholars without actually doing any scholarly work. They are now beginning to discover that their obsession with obsolescent ecclesiastical institutions is losing its market value, and that a younger generation of Catholics could not care less either about the obsolescent institutions or their equally obsolescent critics.

Just as it did not have leaders who could cope with the crisis of the 1960s, so American Catholicism did not have scholars who could interpret the crisis. Those who did shape ideas and opinions were effective at attacking, but quite ineffective at creating. A scholarly tradition is being built in the American Church, but the young scholars remain silent and hesitant; and it may be some time before they are able to push the journalist-intellectuals aside. In the meantime, there will be a notable shortage of vision and hope—creative vision and productive hope—in the American Church.

A third institution that failed is the clergy. While the clergy lack both the power of the bishops and the presumed scholarship of the intellectuals, they are still commissioned to be the leaders of the local Church and the visionaries of the grass roots. At the present time, however, it seems that the American clergy are so caught up in their own problems of identity that they are quite incapable of either leading or prophesying. I am not able at this time to speak in any way about the preliminary findings of the study of the Catholic priesthood being conducted jointly by the National Opinion Research Center at the University of Chicago and the Department of Psychology of Loyola University, but enough other studies have been made to enable me to attempt, on the basis of such studies, some tentative generalizations about the clergy. They are, I must confess, generalizations that many of the clergy will not like.

The excellent study done for the Archdiocese of Hartford by two members of the Psychology Department of Yale University concludes that clergymen tend to be "passive-dependent" personalities.

One must note that in view of the type of person recruited, the seminary training they were submitted to, and the structures in which they were forced to work, one would have been singularly ill-advised to expect any other kind of personality. Many priests have been kept in a state of permanent semi-adolescence. A successful adaptation to the system in which they had to live required that they remain immature. They needed strong leadership and rigid structures to lean on and to hate. Unfortunately, the structures have been knocked aside, and the leadership has lost its credibility. And so these clerics find themselves cast adrift in the sea of ambiguity and confusion.

Furthermore, their personalities show little tolerance for ambiguity or confusion. The situation must be either white or black. Either celibacy is a rigidly required condition for the priesthood, or one must find a wife at once. Either the Church must renew itself overnight, or the cleric must seek relevance somewhere else. Either all questions of priestly identity must be resolved, or a completely new identity must be sought. Either our victories are won tomorrow morning, or we give up and sullenly await defeat. Such a personality is not well disposed to either close co-operation with colleagues or long-range effort.

In addition, there seems to be a strong strain of superficiality in the clergy. They have relatively little in the way of internal convictions (or what in religious terms would be called "faith") and such convictions as they had were in earlier eras propped up by the external structure. Now the external props are gone and there is not much coherent personality core around which a man can organize his life. Affection, support, succor, attention, he desperately needs. He wants to be "liked," but he has precious little to give. He wants to "create a real Christian community," but he has no taste for hard work.

He is therefore given the clichés and the catchwords, such as "community," "secular," and "dialogue." He asks pseudoprofound questions, but provides no answers, not even the beginning of one. When others approach him for help, he is inclined to engage in exhibitionism. He claims to be interested in relationships and ideas, but flees from these relationships when they make any insistent demands on him. And he flips from romantic fashion to romantic fashion, praising now the cursillos, now sensitivity training, now pentecostalism. He enjoys engaging in "honest" discussion, but shies away from acquiring disciplined competence. He is delighted when, in the sensitivity interlude, a priest "breaks down and confesses that he has a mistress," but is quite unconcerned about whether such an experience makes any contribution to the emotional development of the people involved in the sensitivity session.

There are some who argue that this is a caricature of the clergy. They will contend that my portrait of the priest as a rigid and inflexible person, ill-equipped to cope with change—however enthusiastic he may be about the change—is exaggerated and unfair. I am certainly not arguing that my portrait is typical of all priests, though I think the tendencies I described are to be found in many of us, and I would not want to exclude myself from the indictment.

But it is, I think, more important to note that, given the training and work structure in which the clergy lived until very recently, one could hardly expect any other effect. What is surprising is that so many people managed to emerge from such structures with strong and vigorous personalities as in fact did so. When one considers what the clergy had to put up with in years gone by, the amazing thing is that we still do have some leaders and prophets. But in the 1960s we did not have nearly enough of either. New methods of recruiting and training, as well as new structures of work and life, will be required before we do.

The dramatic deterioration of American Catholicism in the 1960s, then, can be attributed to the failure of the three institutions to which Catholics might have looked for both the new values and the new structures to respond to the challenge of the explosive forces pent up in the fifties and released in the sixties. The hierarchy and the intellectuals and the clergy, for reasons rooted in the social history of American Catholicism, were not up to what the task required.

THE 1970S

The 1960s were disastrous for Roman Catholicism in the United States. The exciting and challenging forces released by the Vatican Council, as well as the great hopes stirred up by the Council, have been frustrated. The institution is in disarray and disorder, and seems to be deteriorating as a result. Losses are serious. All this is true, but it does not follow that the losses are fatal or even, as far as the masses of the Catholic population go, very important. The elites are badly disturbed, and this would include at the most a quarter of a million people—priests, religious, those laity that read the *National Catholic Reporter*. The rest of the Catholic population might be mildly upset—some of them because change is going too fast, others because it is going too slow. But the Catholic masses are only marginally touched by the present crisis, a fact that those deeply involved in the crisis find very difficult to accept. It is frequently said to me that research in American Catholicism is foolish, because things are changing so fast that the research is out of date before the findings can be reported. Such an assumption may be true of small groups within the population, but it is rarely true of a large population group, and it is certainly not true (as far as we can determine) of most American Catholics. The various studies available indicate:

a. there is almost no apostasy from Catholicism;

b. the apostasy that does occur is rooted more in personality problems than intellectual doubts;

c. doctrinal orthodoxy and religious devotion in the Catholic population have not changed very much. The change on birth control—which seems to have happened between 1963 and 1965—has affected no more than 20 per cent of the Catholic population, since half of American Catholics were not willing to accept the Church's birth-control position, even in the early 1950s;

d. the United States is a denominational society in which people's religious affiliation and devotion are not linked very closely with anything Church organizational structure or ecclesiastical elites say or do;

e. despite a considerable amount of popular journalism to the contrary, there is no evidence of a "desacralization," much less of a "secularization," in American society—or in any other society, for that matter; quite the contrary: if anything, we are witnessing a return to sacral behavior, frequently in rather bizarre forms.

What will happen to American Catholicism if it loses its school system, what powerful ecclesiastical leadership it has, much of its highly respected clergy, and its ability to impose a distinctive moral system on its adherents? One is forced to conclude that, in the short run, not much. American Protestantism has done quite nicely without any of these structures for a good long time. What would be lost, one suspects, would be a certain amount of energy, vitality, self-confidence, and aggressiveness, which were once characteristic of American Catholicism and which still can be found at the lower-class end of the continuum of American Protestantism. From such a perspective, one could say that the 1960s were the period when Roman Catholicism in the United States began the journey to becoming just another denomination (albeit the largest) in our denominational society—quite indistinguishable, in most of its values and much of its organizational structure, from other upper-middle-class denominations.

Whether such a development is good or bad depends, one supposes, on the perspective of the evaluator. A good case could be made that American society would be somewhat the worse if Roman Catholicism at the end of the century is mostly indistinguishable from Episcopalianism and Methodism.

What we are witnessing, then, is perhaps only a minor disaster. The massive structure of American Catholicism will be changed and transformed, but hardly eliminated. Over the long haul, of course, if the crisis of the 1960s is not resolved, if confusion and chaos and disintegration persist, if new structures and new values do not emerge, then our projection may seem too optimistic. Catholicism in the United States, instead of being comparable to Methodism or

Anglicanism, may be comparable to Catholicism in France. But if one had to choose between these two alternatives as being the more likely for 1980, it would not be wise to bet on the latter alternative.

It would nonetheless be unfortunate both for Catholicism and for American religion in general if the vitality of immigrant Catholicism, which culminated in the dramatic euphoria of the early sessions of the Vatican Council, was to blow itself out as do great tropical storms when they cross land masses. Will the trends we have described be reversed? Will new structures and values emerge while some of the vitality remains? There is, in my judgment, no reason to expect the sudden reversal of the trends that have set in since 1965. The 1970s will probably witness a slow disintegration of the remaining structures of immigrant Catholicism, combined with the slow emergence of new structures and new values. There will continue to be erosion of personnel, resources, and institutions. Many buildings will stand empty or be sold. Many auxiliary firms will go out of business. Many lay people will move to the margins of the Church, still considering themselves Catholic, but taking neither the structure nor its values too seriously. The process will continue to be painful; though perhaps because it is familiar, pain will be less noticeable. The outlook is not for complete disintegration, not even for accelerated deterioration, but rather for a slow and troublesome downhill journey.

There could be a reversal of the trends, of course. A dramatic change in the style of the Papacy might recover the spirit of the early sixties. An ecumenical council that is truly representative of the forces at work in the Church might get us out of the present impasse, and there might be a revolution. By revolution I don't mean a violent attempt to seize by physical force control of the ecclesiastical institution. But I do mean a dramatic move by dissident forces in the Church to obtain some of the tools of ecclesiastical power. Such a move could force, for example, popular election of bishops. Given the fact that, according to our analysis, the laity is largely apathetic, the clergy confused and restless but without direction, and the hierarchy inflexible in its evaluation of the situation, such a power play may seem unlikely. Alienation and disaffection are much easier responses. Nor is there any real reason to think that the revolution would necessarily be a constructive change for the Church. On the other hand, we are living an era of American history when quasi-revolutionary behavior is taken to be quite legitimate. (Witness the display that is put on at the meetings of professional academic associations.) Furthermore, some of the clergy have, in their involvement in the civil rights and peace movements, become quite skillful at the tactics of disruption and harassment. There is always the possibility of large numbers of priests deciding to "call in sick" on Sunday. There is among some clergy, who at one time would have been described as moderate, increased evidence of an "ugly" mood. Disillusioned and disappointed by the failure of their postconciliary dreams, and saddened by the departure from the ranks of the priesthood of colleagues for whom they had great respect and affection, these clergy, not all of them young and not all of them without ecclesiastical positions, have lately been muttering darkly that maybe this is indeed a prerevolutionary period.

There is much in the social-science theorizing about revolution that would suggest that such an event would not be impossible. Revolutions, we are told by those who study them, happen in "j-curve" situations. After a period of dramatic and exciting progress, there follows a leveling off and then a downturn. It is precisely at this downturn that the revolutionary phase begins. According to some observers of American Catholicism, the downturn came with the encyclical letter *Humanae Vitae*. But whether there is the will in American Catholicism, and particularly in its clergy, for a quasi-revolutionary gesture, and whether there will occur a spark that could ignite revolutionary tinder, are questions the answers to which must at the present time remain extremely uncertain.

If a new value system is to emerge during the 1970s, what would it look like?

The first of the basic issues to which the Church must address itself is the question of personal meaning. In most prior societies that mankind has known, meaning systems and culture systems were the same thing; that is to say, each culture provided its own fairly comprehensive interpretive scheme, which enabled those who were part of the culture to interpret the phenomenological reality that impinged on their consciousness. There was a series of propositions that explained what reality was all about—a series of propositions that was practically "given" by the culture. At the present time, however, man shops in a marketplace of meaning systems. Indeed, as Thomas Luckmann has pointed out, meaning systems have become consumer goods.

The Church ought not to be too troubled by this fact. Identification of religion with culture has not particularly helped the Church. The interpretive scheme that man puts together by his own personal free choice (at least more or less so) ought to appear more desirable to the Judaeo-Christian tradition. However, it is necessary for the Church to realize that, to a considerable extent, each new generation has to make its own religious decisions—has to fashion its own interpretive scheme. The search for meaning is no longer something that can be solved once, but is something that each person must solve for himself and that each generation must wrestle with in the context of its own meaningful generational experiences.

One supposes that such a situation has been true of the Western world for perhaps a century, but there is a new variable at work at present which presents an extraordinarily interesting challenge to the churches. Not only have the old gods failed, but the new gods have failed, too. Science, orthodox Marxism, liberal political philosophy, and the pursuit of economic affluence seem to be almost as much in disarray, as meaning systems, as does traditional orthodoxy. The younger generation tells us that the Great God Science has failed because it has not brought peace or justice to the world. Substantial numbers of them have rejected what they think of as the bureaucratic irresponsibility of the organized, computerized, secularized society. They prefer the existentialist loneliness of the hippie groups, the utopian communities, the Zen monasteries, to the rational society. Still others turn for self-fulfillment to group dynamics, attempting to relate "honestly" and "authentically" to their fellow men in the raw emotionality of confrontation, encounter, sensitivity, and therapy groups.

Not only is the search for meaning and value a new one in every generation, but in the present generation it would seem that the presumption is against any of the pre-existing substantive meaning systems, and that personal meaning, if any, has to be found apart from these systems and perhaps in revolt against them.

Another complicating factor is the resurrection experience of the therapeutic process. It is not my intention, surely, to endorse psychoanalysis as the only god that has not failed—its own failures and inadequacies are all too patent; much less am I enthusiastic about the current cult of group dynamics or the arrogant new priesthood of T-group "trainers." But whatever one may say of abuses and extremes, it is still true that psychoanalysis has made possible considerable personal growth for many people, a growth that involves death and resurrection—a putting off of the old man and the putting on of the new—an experience that has its own horrors even worse than the horrors of physical death. There is now the theoretical possibility that a person never need stop expanding his personality. Enrichment and development and fulfillment of the human person can continue for decades, though always through a death-and-resurrection process. Kenneth Keniston sees the maturation process going on in some young people at least until they are thirty, and other researchers view the identity-crisis years from thirty-five to forty-five as being the most critical and also potentially the most productive in a person's life. Personal fulfillment, then, is at least part of the raw material of any new interpretive scheme, and is, indeed, raw material that has profound religious implications.

What are the implications for the structure of the Church in the present state of man's perennial search for meaning? How ought the Church to react when it observes that the new gods seem to be as dead as the old, and that now for each new generation the meaning quest must start anew? One would think that the first reaction to such a phenomenon would be to rejoice, for once again the religious interpretive schemes can claim some kind of legitimacy as potential meaning systems. The epistemology of science is no longer powerful enough to rule them out on a priori grounds. There ought to be even more rejoicing when it is noted that the issue of death and resurrection and the issue of transcendence seem to be once more among the principal issues that must be faced. The Church which sees mankind engaged in two pilgrimages—one toward the omega point and the other toward self-fulfillment—and realizes that in fact these two pilgrimages are one, ought to realize that its strategic position is at the present time quite good. As Brian Wicker has pointed out, the Church can, if it so desires, provide an answer to the one question that humanism cannot answer: what does death do to man's quest for self-fulfillment? Religion is not only free once again to compete in the open marketplace of interpretive schemes; it can also provide a high-quality product, a product toward which there seems to be a sustained predisposition in substantial numbers of mankind.

In the previous paragraphs we noted that the quest for meaning was intimately connected with the quest for self-fulfillment—that indeed they are the same quest, for modern man. As Erik Erikson has observed, you cannot have an identity without ideology. One can become oneself only with, through, and for others. Hence, the second critical issue that the Church must face is modern man's quest for community. Whether there is more or less intimacy, warmth, and self-support in contemporary urban industrial society than there was in the peasant communes of the past, may be open to question. What is not open to question is the fact that modern man possesses both the affluence and the vocabulary to engage in a highly self-conscious quest for community and for intimacy. The hippie communes, the underground churches, "educational villages," encounter and marathon groups (clothed or unclothed), are all manifestations of a much more widespread phenomenon—the search for openness, honesty, and trust in human relationships.

There are many dangers in the quest for community. Community does not, as many people think, happen. It requires hard work. Nor is it something, at least normally, that emerges as the result of self-conscious search. Rather, it is the frequently unintended result of common effort. Furthermore, many of the enthusiastic searchers for community fail to face the obvious historical truth that community usually dominates individuality and eliminates privacy. In any conflict between individual and community in mankind's past, community has won. Community now has at its disposal all the elaborate techniques of group dynamics to increase its power and to dominate and manipulate its members. Finally, there does not yet seem to be much awareness among the cultists of community of the problem of the Oedipus complex and of the regression of members of the intimate community to behavior out of their familial past. Most of us know only one kind of intimate relationship—that which we learned in our own families. Hence, when we are faced with a new set of intense and intimate relationships, we fall back on the paradigmatic behavior patterns of the past and convert our colleagues in the community into parents or siblings, with results that are disastrous for all concerned.

But for all the risks and dangers in the quest for community, mankind is not likely to turn away from it, for we have always dreamed of the possibility of trusting love with one another. Modern psychology, for all its inadequacies, brought us much closer to that goal. The bizarre aberrations that show up on the fringes of the quest for community are merely evidence of how intense the quest is.

And what can the Church say in response to the news that men want to love one another more, and that new insights into the human personality seem to be facillitating that desire for greater love? What can the Church say upon discovering that its members want greater trust in their relationships with one another? What in particular can the Church say in response to the quest for community—the Church whose founder told it, "By this shall all men know that you are my disciples, that you have love for one another"? Yet in fact, the Church, when it has not been opposed to psychology, has at least been skeptical of the quest for community among its membership. The underground ecclesiastical groups are underground precisely because the aboveground congregations look with suspicion upon small, informal, and intimate ecclesiastical groups. The large urban or suburban congregation is a marvelous escape from intimacy and trust. The amount of love for one another to be discovered in such congregations is minimal, and no demand is made that people risk themselves in close relationship with their fellow believers. Heaven protect us from a situation in which the warmth and intimacy of our love for one another *really would* make us stand out as being different from the rest of the human race. The conventionalization—not to say the "embourgeoisement"—of relationships in the Church is not merely an inadequate response to contemporary man's quest for community; it is, even worse, a false witness to the genius of Christianity.

The sexual relationship is the paradigm of all human relationships, and the marriage community is the paradigm of all human communities. The fear that stands in the way of trust is strongest in that most intimate of relationships; and the payoff of trust and openness is the greatest in the sexual relationship, since it is reinforced by the possibility of overwhelming physical pleasure. Yet the resistance to trust, openness, and friendship is also extraordinarily powerful. Shame over one's sexuality, which is apparently basically the same as uncertainty about one's own sexual identity, stands as a powerful barrier to openness between man and woman, a barrier that is deeply rooted in the unresolved problems of one's relationship with one's parents. The battle between the drive toward physical and psychological unity on the one hand, and shame and self-hatred on the other, is typical of the whole human condition, but most painful and also potentially most pleasurable in the sexual relationship. If man can learn to live in loving and trusting concern with his mate, then he probably will have no trouble in living in openness and trust with anyone else.

But more must be said. While the husband-and-wife relationship is the paradigm of all human relationships, and while the sexuality between husband and wife may very well provide the raw material that makes possible other intimate friendships, it must further be said that there is a strong sexual component in all human intimacy, since intimacy involves the total man, body and spirit, and man's body cannot escape (and obviously ought not to want to escape) its sexuality. Sex, then, is not only the paradigm of all human relationships, but also permeates all human relationships. The relationship of pupil and teacher has profoundly sexual implications, as Socrates and Alcibiades were aware. The teacher—or at least the good teacher

—to some extent seduces the personality of his student in order that he might attract the student to his ideas. The priest, prophet, charismatic leader, therapist—all engage in relationships that, at least when we stop to think about it, are powerfully sexual in their color and tone. Similarly, other human friendships, between members of the same sex and across sexual lines, which are not marital and are not aimed at sexual intercourse, nonetheless are deeply rooted in the sexuality of the friendship partners. The relevant question is not whether all human relationships are sexual, but rather, what the implications for human relationships are of our new insight into the pervasiveness of sexuality.

The Freudian revolution took place only yesterday. For several thousand years the Platonist and Manichee temptation was dominant. Sex was viewed as something that pertained to the body, which, in its turn, imprisoned the human spirit. Sexuality was, then, at best a drag on the human spirit, and at worst, according to St. Augustine, a sin, even between married partners. The Freudian insight overthrew the Platonist and Manichee tradition: sex is not a drag on the human spirit, but a stimulus to it. It does not retard human growth, but rather drives men forward toward growth (and incidentally, also, on occasion, toward destruction). The human race has only begun to assimilate the implications of this astonishing revolution, and the revolution has precious little to do with Jane Fonda on the cover of *Newsweek* or *Oh! Calcutta!* on Broadway, or any of the alleged new "permissiveness" in American society.

One would have thought, given the attitudes of the scriptures about sexuality and the pervasive sexual imagery used to describe the relationship between God and His people, that Christianity would have been delighted by the Freudian insight. At least some of the churches have not been so delighted, but others have thought that the appropriate response was to develop arguments suggesting that almost every type of sexual perversion was not only not sinful, but positively healthy. These two reactions probably are characteristic forms of guilt repression; the churches have been very guilty on the subject of sex. They allowed themselves to be conquered by the Platonist-Manichee temptation. Despite the clear evidence of the scriptures, they have persisted in seeing man as a dualistic creature and viewing his body and his sexuality as something of which to be ashamed. That the Roman Catholic Church, which uses the powerful and obvious intercourse symbol in its Holy Saturday liturgy, emphasizing that the Resurrection is best symbolized by the sexual act, can respond to the Freudian revolution with nothing more adequate than the encyclical letter *Humanae Vitae*, is a sign of how profound the guilt in Roman Catholicism is over its own weakness in the face of the Manichee tradition. The love of Christ for His Church is so intertwined in the New Testament with the love of husband for wife that one simply cannot understand how the Roman Church or any Christian church, for that matter, could possibly not rejoice in the Freudian revolution. However, it may take us a while yet to purge the Manichee guilt out of our bodies ecclesiastical.

The implication of the Freudian revolution for the Church is perfectly clear, though when it stands in all its nakedness (to use an appropriate term), it becomes terrifying to many virtuous Christians, not excluding their even more virtuous leaders: *sexual love must be the model for all relationships in the Church.*

If the relationship between Christ and His people is thus compared to the relationship between husband and wife, the dictum we have just stated should not be surprising. Yet, surprising it surely is. Who could think, for example, of the relationship between a bishop and a pastor, a pastor and an assistant, a religious superior and (you should excuse the expression) his subject, as being modeled after the love of man for a woman? Who would think that the members of a Christian congregation should strive to treat each other with the gentleness, respect, affection, concern, patience, and tenderness that is absolutely essential if the sexual payoff in marriage is not going to quickly deteriorate? Who could possibly think that the relationship of respect, encouragement, and reinforcement obvious in good marriages should be demanded from all assemblies of the people of God? Who, indeed, would think that Jesus ought to be taken literally when He says, "By this shall all men know that you are my disciples, that you have love for one another"?

Contemporary man is seeking for unity not only with himself, not only with those around him, not only especially with his mate, but also for unity with the physical world in which he is immersed. He wants to once again recapture—or perhaps capture for the first time—a sense of oneness with his own emotions and with the basic forces of the universe that he feels surge up in his emotions. Rock music, drugs, hippie culture, the new quest for the sacred, are all, in their own ways, revolts against the hyperrationalism of the hyper-secularized Cartesian society, and attempts (however limited in their success) to establish contact with the primal life forces. Not on the fringes of the secular society, but at its very core in the great universities, we find young men and women beginning to lead monastic lives, searching for gurus, seeking for the Holy, giving themselves over to contemplation, detachment, and solitude, withdrawing from the "rat race" in order that they may maintain perspective on themselves and on the life they live. Yet other young people are donning strange robes we can only call vestments, developing new kinds of liturgy that frequently are merely re-enactments of such old liturgies as witchcraft, and relying on tarot cards, the *I Ching*, and the signs of the zodiac as symbols that will bring them in touch with the primordial forces of the universe. In other words, they are trying to break through the tyranny of the superego and the ego to come into contact with the preconscious and the unconscious, for therein they expect they will find some sort of meaning, some sort of belonging, and some sort of unity with the primal forces in which we all find ourselves immersed.

The mystical and the liturgical are different from one another, and much that is now passing for both mystical and liturgical is, in fact, neither. But the quest for ecstasy, achieved with or without artificial help, and either by Dionysian or Apollonian methods, seems to be almost as old as mankind. Even though such masters of ancient traditions of the liturgical and the mystical as the Catholic Church seem to have abandoned both traditions, the traditions are still very much alive. One wonders, in passing, how many Catholics know a mystic, much less an ecstatic.

Reason rules over man's hunger for the mystical and the orgiastic only as a constitutional monarch. The pentecostal hysteria, rock

Mass, folk music, guitars, to say nothing of astrology, divination, and oriental mysticism are all a judgment on the Western churches for their failure to respond to man's yearning for the sacred and the ecstatic. The Church once again did not have the courage to believe in itself or the best of its own traditions. It thought that there was no room for the mystical in an age of science or for the sacred in an age of reason. Now, when the mystical and the sacred reappear, and with a vengeance, the Church is caught off guard. It had always argued that not by cold reason alone does man live, and now finds itself surprised to learn that it was right.

In summary, then, the challenges for Church structure in years to come are to be found in man's search for personal meaning, for love and intimacy, for a more profound appreciation of sexuality, and for closer unity with the primal forces of the universe. These are challenges that the Church ought to welcome, because they are challenges that speak to the best of its own traditions—but to the elements of these traditions in which the Church itself seems to have regrettably lost some confidence.

So much, then, for the areas in which one might reasonably hope that Catholicism might discover or rediscover a vital system of values. In passing, I might note that Roman Catholicism, if it develops values of the sort that I have mentioned, could make an extremely important contribution to American society. It would be high time.

What new institutions seem to be emerging that might reinforce such values? It would be my judgment that four different kinds of institutions could engage in shaping the organizational structures of Catholicism in the 1970s and probably even more in the 1980s: priests' associations, small-group ecclesiastical communities, reformed religious orders, and Catholic educational institutions (particularly colleges and universities).

The priests' association is a uniquely American contribution to Roman Catholicism. Other countries have had priests' associations in the past, but the style, vigor, and short-range effectiveness of the American priests' associations is characteristically American. The associations were quite successful during the 1960s in winning basic concessions for their members. Personnel boards, retirement boards, trade unions, increased wages, some sort of protection of basic human rights—all have been achieved in many dioceses with fantastic speed, given the resistance that such ideas would have encountered a few years before. The leaders of the priests' associations tend to be pragmatic, efficient, consensus-oriented people. They are not revolutionaries or visionaries. Their ideas of how the Church ought to be restructured are limited, and their vision of the future of the Church hardly very exciting. Indeed, their national journal is almost embarrassingly clubby and seems to share with the diocesan press an apparently incurable ecclesiastical tendency to print pictures of its top leaders. Furthermore, priests'-association leadership is very wary about being criticized by its rank-and-file membership and venturing beyond the clearest mandates that the membership is willing to give. On the other hand, the federation of priests' associations does represent a potentially very powerful structure. If it ever should fall into the hands of a leadership that combines vision with political astuteness, American Catholicism would be in for some extraordinary days.

The underground communities, which are apparently proliferating at a fantastic rate (in one large archdiocese that I know of, it is alleged that there are more than two hundred of them), are a far more subtle influence on the Church. Granted the peril of agnosticism, hyperemotionalism, and faddism, the emergence of these sect-like groups, who refuse to break with the organized Church but also refuse to be constrained by the official structures of that Church, is fascinating and potentially very important. The great reform movements from the past history of Christianity—the Franciscans, the Benedictines, and the Brothers and Sisters of the Common Life, for example—all began in just this fashion. At their best, the members of the underground communities seek not less religion, but more; not an easier faith, but a more challenging one; not a simple liturgy, but a more inspiring one; not priests who are more worldly, but rather ones who are more holy; not the friendship of cocktail parties, but serious and deep relationships by which all men might know whose disciples they are. One supposes that only a very small minority of Catholic laity are part of such underground communities and that many of those who do belong are not interested in attempting to modify the institutional Church about whose reform they have pretty much despaired. And yet, like the priests' associations, they represent a potential for power and energy that is very difficult to ignore. Many of them are likely to be torn by aggression and transference neurosis. But those who survive such crises will be groups of human beings that the organized Church will have to reckon with.

A third group of institutions whose influence is likely to increase in the 1970s are the reformed religious orders. Many religious communities of women, and some of men, have gone through drastic modifications in the closing years of the past decade. In the process, they have suffered heavy losses. Some religious have left because the changes have not come quickly enough; others because too many changes came too quickly; and still others because, while they worked for change, they found that their personality structures could not cope with the free-wheeling communities that emerged from change. Yet one merely has to visit some of the "experimental" houses of these reformed religious orders to realize that a great deal of vital energy exists in such communities and that it is frequently combined with a good deal of theoretical and psychological sophistication. I have a hunch that such communities are going to be increasingly attractive to young people in the years to come—not perhaps to as many who used to join religious communities, and certainly to a rather different kind of young person. But they, too, well may be a power that must be reckoned with.

Finally, I would advise those interested in the emerging institutions in the Catholic Church to keep a close eye on the campuses of Catholic colleges and universities. Self-hatred and inferiority feelings are still rampant at these institutions. They are also subject to being swept by fashion—the two most recent fashions being the selection of lay boards of trustees and the appointment of non-Catholics as college presidents. But in the midst of the present turmoil in American higher education, at least some of the more sophisticated Catholic educators are beginning to realize that they have three of the things that the radicals seem to demand in American higher educational institutions—values, community, and concern about the total person. If enough Catholic educators can overcome their inferiority complexes, they may begin to realize that Catholic higher education can make an important contribution, not only to the rest of American higher education but to the Church itself. Both these contributions, alas, are rather minimal at the present time.

What then, in conclusion, are the future prospects for American Catholicism? The long-range outlook is obscure, though one can assert with reasonable confidence that American Catholicism will survive. The next decade or two is likely to witness more erosion; then new structures and values will begin to evolve, with the possibility that evolution will be accelerated either by revolutionary interludes or by major change in the government of the universal Church.

The outlook, then, is at best guarded, and probably somewhat pessimistic. But it is not necessarily so. There are many things one would not have expected in the middle of the 1950s. John XXIII was one, and the Second Vatican Council was another. Sociological analysis, I think, must despair of the possibility of finding explanations for either event. The sociologist would content himself with saying that Pope John and the Council were both "idiosyncratic." The man of faith may wish to use another word.

Table 1.
Catholic Statistics 1949–69*

	1949	1959	1969
Priests	42,334	52,689	59,620
Sisters	141,606	164,922	167,167
Seminarians	26,215	38,105	33,990
Converts	117,113	140,411	102,845
Elementary schools	2,450,222	4,505,475	3,926,080
Secondary schools	508,724	810,769	1,115,351
Colleges	240,048	290,769	435,716

* Source: *The Official Catholic Directory.* New York: P. J. Kenedy & Sons, 1969.

Table 2.

*Gains and Losses in Catholic Population in
1959 and 1969, Assuming 1949 Proportions as a Base*

	1959	1969
Priests	5,275*	7,465*
Sisters	6,324	−7,290†
Seminarians	9,793	−3,098
Elementary schools	678,622	1,412
Secondary schools	121,990	219,421
Colleges	27,706	66,448
Converts	11,587	−38,861

* Figure indicates number in excess of what would be required to maintain ratio of priests to population over twenty-five in 1949.

† Figure equals number of sisters who would have been required to bring ratio to 1949 level.

Table 3.

*Gains and Losses in Catholic Population in
1969, Assuming 1959 Proportions as a Base*

Priests	1,663
Sisters	−14,247
Seminarians	−15,927
Elementary schools	−295,368
Secondary schools	12,706
Colleges	22,685
Converts	−51,607

9. The Adolescent Church

From a sociological point of view, the most obvious thing that can be said about American Catholicism is that it is upwardly mobile, that it is rapidly becoming the church of the suburban middle class, as it leaves behind its origins and its roots in the urban immigrant ghetto. This transition from slum to suburbia is such an overwhelmingly obvious facet of American Catholic life that it is frequently overlooked (if not denied) in any discussion of the problems that the American Church faces today. There are few phenomena in contemporary Catholic life in the United States that cannot be explained by the fact that the transition from slums to suburbia has occurred at almost exactly the same time that by good chance or bad chance the universal Church is moving from the post-Tridentine to the post-Vatican age. American Catholicism thus is caught in the intersection of two transitions, and the euphoria and excitement as well as the tension and discouragement of the present moment are, for the most part, the result of this fascinating, albeit frightening, intersection of transitions.

The effect of the socioeconomic transformation of American Catholicism should be so obvious that one hardly need document it. Nonetheless, the transition has been seriously questioned by two groups of people—by anti-Catholics (whether they be masquerading as social scientists or not) who would contend that the failure of Catholics to be imbued with the "Protestant ethic" inhibits their acclimation to American society, and by the liberal Catholic critics who feel that their own position would be seriously weakened if it could be established that despite their theories, American Catholics were indeed becoming part of the mainstream of American life. Hence, it is necessary to provide some documentation for the change that we claim has occurred.

TABLE 1. SOCIOECONOMIC STATUS BY RELIGION AND AGE*

Per Cent	Age 23–29 Protestant	Catholic	Age 30–39 Protestant	Catholic	Age 40–49 Protestant	Catholic	Age 50–59 Protestant	Catholic
Attending college	29	28	34	26	29	19	25	12
In Duncan categories 6–10†	32	30	40	32	36	19	40	31
Earning more than $8000	29	25	40	36	51	39	40	29
(N)	(907)	(352)	(167)	(653)	(169)	(691)	(97)	(352)

* The Protestants in the sample are white Protestants who have the same geographic distribution as do the Catholics, so that there is built in a control in the table for city size, area of the country, and race.

† See Otis D. Duncan, "A Socioeconomic Index for all Occupations," in Albert J. Reiss, Jr., *Occupations and Social Status*. New York: Free Press, 1961, ch. 6.

While Protestants in their fifties were twice as likely to go to college as Catholics, and Protestants in their thirties and forties were ten percentage points more likely to have gone to college than Catholics, among the younger generation those Catholics in their twenties (at least in 1963, when the data were collected) are just as likely to have gone to college as are Protestants of comparable age.

Similarly, while Protestants in their thirties, forties, and fifties are much more likely to be members of the upper-middle or upper class than Catholics, amongst the younger generation there is again no difference. Finally, Catholics in their twenties and thirties are not significantly less likely to earn more than $8000 than their Protestant fellow Americans, although in the forty-plus age bracket the economic achievement of Catholics was substantially less than their Protestant counterparts. In other words, those Catholics who were born after the beginning of the New Deal are economically, educationally, and occupationally indistinguishable from their fellow Americans.

Transition can be neatly summed up by saying that in the Catholic adult population between twenty-three and sixty, 50 per cent are either immigrants or the children of immigrants, but among those in their twenties the Catholics are as likely to go to college and to succeed economically as are the Protestants. It is fair to assume, therefore, that in another twenty or twenty-five years, at all age levels Catholics and Protestants will be socioeconomically indistinguishable from each other.

But if the change is going on, it is equally clear that the change is not over, and the fact of change will explain both many of the weaknesses of the past (the absence of scholarship, defensiveness, fear of innovation, reluctance to face the problems of the contemporary world) and also the tensions and the difficulties of the present, because while American Catholicism is in the process of leaving behind its past, it has yet to achieve the maturity that there is at least some reason to hope the future might hold. Indeed, it is very useful for us to think of American Catholicism as going through its period of adolescence at the present time. It is no longer the infant Church of the immigrant era, but it is yet to become the mature adult Church that finds itself securely accepted in American society. It is, in this time of its adolescence, becoming conscious of itself and self-conscious, and like all other adolescents, it is seeking an explanation for itself as it struggles through the period of identity crisis. Unfortunately, as Philip Gleason, the distinguished Catholic historian, has pointed out, American Catholicism is going through its identity crisis in a state of amnesia about its own past.

Without pushing things too far, we can use the analogy of adolescence to order many of the phenomena to be observed in contemporary Catholic life. First of all, the adolescent tends to be restless, moody, and at times rebellious. Where previously we had a quiet, passive, and frequently docile child, we have the adolescent —a mercurial and unpredictable creature who may at one time be riding the crests of euphoria and at another time sink to the depths of pessimism and despair. One need not travel far in the American Church today to discover that moodiness and restlessness are abroad in the land. Several years ago, I had the occasion, as part of a study for the Carnegie Foundation, to visit some thirty Catholic university campuses to speak not only to people on campus, but to other Catholics in the areas where the schools were located. The tension was so thick in most of the places we visited you could almost cut it with a knife. Some schools, some dioceses, some religious communities, were as charged with enthusiasm as teen-agers at a rock and roll dance, while in other situations (and, I fear, far-more-numerous ones) the combination of sullenness and despair was so powerful that one expected an explosion almost momentarily. "It's too good to be true" was heard almost as frequently as "If *they* don't change things pretty quickly we're going to get out." Not only is the Church as an institution affected, but the adolescence of the total institution seems to manifest itself in the behavior of subgroups within the institution and even of individual members. American Catholicism is impatient, and those who must deal with it in positions of responsibility and authority would be ill-advised to think that simply advising people on the need for patience is going to solve the problem. Indeed, the advice to remain patient, one very much fears, is only calculated to make present tension-filled situations even worse.

Secondly, like all adolescents, American Catholicism is profoundly angry. The adolescent is very angry at the world around him, because he feels cheated, cheated both of the innocent joys of his youth and also of the adulthood that was denied him in his youth, and is being denied him presently. Just as the adolescent is likely to act out his anger in aggressive and at times violent behavior, so there is much aggressiveness to be observed across the length and breadth of American Catholicism. By no means the most powerful anger is to be found in the strident (and at times vicious) articles and editorials in certain sections of the Catholic press. Indeed, such anger is usually quite mild compared to what one can hear in conversations, particularly among younger lay people and among religious and priests of almost every age. One very much fears that if those in leadership positions do not recognize the ferocity of this anger and need to placate it by at least an honest exchange of ideas, the anger, like all adolescent anger, will become more powerful and self-destructive.

Thirdly, American Catholicism, like every adolescent, is shallow, superficial, and unscholarly, swept by catchwords, such as "kerygmatic," "relevance," "diaspora," "encounter," "experience," and "dialogue." Intellectual fads and fashions combine with the catchwords to create an unstable ideology that is not only a substitute for scholarship and for thought but actually a pretext for rejecting precise scholarship and serious intellectual investigation. American Catholicism is going through an era in which its ideology is being fashioned by Renaissance Men, who are instant experts on all questions and whose opinions on war and peace, birth control, celibacy, Catholic education, lay/clergy relationships, sex, and the future of the Church are as unquestionable and unchallengeable as they are undocumentable and untrue. These instant experts need no more evidence than their assertions and no more credentials than their names. He who dares to produce research evidence against such infallible teaching authority is accused of dishonesty, conservatism, or having "sold out." Yet, because of the absence of more serious scholarship and of any sense of historical identity, American Catholicism listens eagerly to the coffeehouse wisdom of the self-appointed instant expert. Ironically, it is precisely these experts whose approach to reality is so profoundly anti-intellectual who substantiate their own charge that American Catholicism is itself anti-intellectual. They are products of the very crimes they criticize. Presumably, this period of governance by journalists will not last long, and the developing scholarly concern with the theology, sociology, and history of the American Church will provide a depth that we lack in our present adolescent superficiality. However, the scholars of the future should not expect that the universally knowledgeable journalists will easily yield their positions. For just as adolescents are rigidly intolerant of dissent, so many of the so-called Catholic liberals are not sufficiently liberal to permit others to disagree with them, and many of the self-critics are far too sensitive to permit others to criticize them.

Fourthly, American Catholicism, like every adolescent, is suffering from a massive inferiority complex. As one of my Jewish colleagues noted to me, "The difference between you and us is that we know we have an inferiority complex and we allow for it. But you people aren't even aware of your own self-hatred." That which is Dutch or German or French or even Chilean is good and praiseworthy and imitable and to be written up in our journals, but that which is American is only worthy of criticism and contempt. The other churches around the world have done great things, and we have wasted our time building schools. The other churches are engaged in mammoth campaigns to reclaim the lost working class, and we haven't even had the guts to lose the working class yet. The other churches are struggling to find their role in a diaspora situation, and we haven't even been honest enough to force ourselves into a diaspora. The other churches are beginning ecumenical dialogue, and we don't know anything about living with non-Catholics. If anyone dares to mention that American Catholicism has accomplished some pretty impressive things, he is ridiculed or accused of aspiring to the hierarchy.

Like all adolescents in their self-rejection and self-hatred, American Catholicism seeks to identify with other and more-impressive brands of Catholicity. In the immediate postwar era it was French Catholicism; then, in the 1950s and the early 1960s it was the German Church we were to adulate and imitate. It would appear from the Catholic press in more recent years that it is the Dutch Church that we should turn to for guidance and inspiration. Since we don't have any theologians of our own, or at least none worth listening to, it follows that the European theological giants become almost mythical hero figures in American Catholicism, and that upon their arrival to dispense truth on our shores we convert them into the standard kind of American hero—the mass-media "personality." And we go to the "conferences" at which they appear, not so much to listen critically as to adore. Rubbing shoulders with these greats becomes a religious experience of incalculable value. Thus, one bright young thing remarked to me, "At one of the discussion groups I actually sat right next to Karl Rahner." Since she spoke no German and Father Rahner speaks little English, one wonders how much "relevance" there was in the "encounter." I must confess I responded with several vulgar words and the suggestion that she ought to think it a far greater honor to be in the auditorium with John Courtney Murray, but, alas, I should have saved my breath.

Fifthly, just as the adolescent is "hung up" on authority figures, simultaneously hating them and being fascinated by them, so the American Church is caught in a real authority problem. It is those very journals and those very individuals (lay and clerical) that are the most vociferous in declaring their independence of authority, that are also the most pathologically interested in the doings of authority. The very people who claim they are completely free of fear of authority figures are the ones whose conversation is filled with references to such figures. It is impossible for an adolescent to be at ease with authority, to be neither frightened by it nor unduly concerned about what it is doing, to leave to authority its own role without having to either fight with it or grovel in its presence. Like all adolescents, American Catholicism can't live with authority, but neither can it live without it.

But perhaps too much has been said about the negative side of adolescence. American Catholicism shares with the adolescent his charm, his enthusiasm, his generosity, his ambition, and his great dreams of the future. If the American Church is confused at the present time, it also clearly has great potential. If it rejects its own past, it has still begun the scholarship that will enable it to understand its past. If it is "hung up" on authority, it has also begun to reorganize and restructure the use of authority. If it is restless and rebellious and moody, it is also (and in this respect it is typically American) not afraid of the future. If it is shallow (and once again it behaves in typically American fashion), it has begun to organize a massive campaign to acquire depth. If it has an identity crisis, it is also in the process of seeking the therapeutic experience to resolve the crisis. But just as maturity does not automatically occur for the adolescent, just as the identity crisis is not automatically solved, so there is no infallible guarantee that American Catholicism is going to survive its present critical times with its potential unstunted and undamaged. The present transitional period, to which social mobility has contributed so much, need not be successfully concluded. On the contrary, when I, like other adolescents, become moody and grim, I am inclined to think that it is possible that American Catholicism, before it grows up, is going to have to go through a period that could charitably be described only as a time of juvenile delinquency.

It would be no exaggeration to say that the decisions of the next two to five years may well affect the future of the American Church for a century, and I would like to devote the remaining pages of this chapter to delineating several of the areas in which decisions must be made and in which decisions are of extraordinarily critical importance.

First of all, there is the apparently grave crisis in religious vocations—a crisis that has to do not merely with the recruitment of personnel into the religious life, but also with perseverance through the seminary or scholasticate, and affiliation with the priestly or religious function after ordination or profession. It is hard to say whether the recruitment or the defection problem is the more serious. Both, however, are quite serious indeed, and the predictions of informed and sensitive observers that if something is not done, and done soon, we may be faced with a vanishing priesthood or a disappearing religious life, are by no means to be taken lightly. It would seem that only the most drastic revision and renewal in both the priesthood and the religious life can possibly avert an extremely severe vocation shortage. Whether such drastic renewal is going to take place must surely be considered problematic. In its absence, it could very well be that the United States would once again, at least from the vocation viewpoint, become a missionary country.

Secondly, it would be idle to pretend that we do not have a very serious problem in Catholic education. The research that my colleagues and I at NORC have carried on indicates that, at least objectively speaking, Catholic schools are doing rather well. They do have at least a reasonable influence on religious and social behavior of Catholics who have gone through them. They are still very popular with the vast majority of American Catholics. But there is no denying that there has been a collapse of confidence in Catholic education, and this collapse has occurred for the most part within the system itself. It is the teachers in Catholic schools—grammar schools, high schools, and colleges—who have lost confidence in themselves. The drumfire of criticism in the Catholic liberal press (and more recently in the non-Catholic press) has created a major identity crisis for Catholic educators, and one only needs to attend their meetings to find that they are running scared and disillusioned. If Catholic educators and the opinion makers among the liberal laity are not persuaded in the very near future that a) Catholic education can make a major and important contribution to the ecumenical church, and that b) the schools have begun to make such a contribution, then it is to be very much feared that the collapse of confidence within the Catholic educational system is going to get worse rather than better.

Thirdly, we must face up honestly to the problem of the "crisis of faith" among young people. Admittedly, this crisis affects only a rather small minority of young Catholics, but the minority that is affected is a crucial minority: the concerned, the enthusiastic, the dedicated—those who could be, in years to come, the lay leaders envisaged by documents of the Vatican Council. It is not the ordinary Catholic or even the indifferent Catholic in his or her early twenties who finds it difficult to reconcile the Church with his notion of the Gospels. It is rather the most sensitive, the most perceptive, the most intelligent, and the most generous of our younger generation who are troubled. Unless we recognize the necessity of re-interpreting our faith in terms that the new breed can find "relevant and authentic," then we shall be faced with the grim possibility of losing them, if not to apostasy, at least to a permanent alienation from the organized Church. It sometimes seems our only response to the unique religious needs of our most intelligent young people is to attempt to put severe restrictions on the use of guitars at Mass. Exciting and challenging liturgy is not the only thing they need, but if we're not willing to engage in the liturgical innovation necessary to capture the imagination of youth, then we might just as well write off the younger generation. And if we don't, then they'll write us off.

Fourthly, we must recognize how low is the morale in many of our dioceses, seminaries, and religious communities. We hear much in the Catholic press of the morale problems of the lay faculty in Catholic colleges, but in my grand tour of Catholic higher education last winter I found the morale of the clerical faculty far lower than that of the lay faculty. The religious and priests, whether they be young or old, are finding themselves caught in their own personal identity crises, not sure what their priesthood or religious life means any more, not persuaded that they haven't wasted their lives, and not certain what they ought to be doing with the years ahead of them. When they look to their leaders for inspiration and guidance, for ingenuity and imagination in implementing the work of the Council, they find frequently only warnings and fears and restrictions and insensitivity and negations. These priests and religious will not leave their vocations; they will not openly rebel; they will not even write letters of protest to the *National Catholic Reporter*. But their happiness, their efficiency, their effectiveness, will be sadly impaired, and the potential of some of our best personnel will be wasted. The challenge for our leaders is clear. Either something must be done about the sagging morale of the clergy and religious, or days of deep and dark frustration are ahead.

Furthermore, a spirit of laicism, or anti-clericalism, is growing in a certain segment of the population. There are two different manifestations of this spirit: one of them harmless if rather stupid, and the other, in my judgment, extremely dangerous. The harmless laicism (and some of the strongest laicists and anti-clericalists in the country are priests and religious) is that which holds that the solution to almost every problem is to turn things over to the laity. Is the Catholic press inefficient? Ah, then we must hire lay editors. Do Catholic colleges have trouble? Then the solution is to establish lay boards of trustees and select lay presidents. Are there problems in diocesan administration? Then the bishop must hire laymen to straighten them out. Must the Vatican Council be implemented at the grass roots? The answer: elect committees of laity representing each parish in the city, and let them apply the council to their own lives. And the truth, of course, is that the laity are not necessarily any better than the clergy at solving any problems that the Church faces, and while laity should be systematically excluded from no problem area in the Church, neither is there any automatic guarantee that their inclusion will solve anything. The lay administrators currently functioning in some Catholic higher educational institutions are no better, and are frequently worse, than some of the clerics. And there is no guarantee that the laymen who might become trustees of these colleges would necessarily avoid the mistakes the clerical trustees are presently making. Just as the clerical status is no substitute for competence, neither is the lay status, and the only criteria that ought to be used for appointment to a position of responsibility in the Church should be competence. The laity as the magic answer to ecclesiastic problems simply doesn't exist.

But the other form of anti-clericalism is far more serious and seems to me to consist essentially of a hatred for the priesthood and a conviction that only when the priestly caste is destroyed will laity be able to emerge in the Church. Even though it's a good thing to discuss ecclesiastical celibacy, and even though in the minds of some of the discussants the question is freedom rather than anti-clericalism, in all too many instances the argument seems to imply a negation of the manhood and the humanity of the celibate priest, and the violence and harshness of the attack seems to mask but slightly the intention to attack and degrade the priesthood in every possible way. I might note in passing that a Freudian psychoanalyst would find it very interesting that some of the most vociferous leaders of the attack on the celibate clergy are ex-seminarians.

It would seem to me, therefore, if major changes cannot be made in the whole structure of lay/clerical relations in the next several years, then the anti-clericalism I have discussed will become more serious, especially since I detected in the college students I interviewed last year an increasing contempt for the clerical administrators of their colleges as well as for a good number of their clerical teachers (especially the teachers of traditional theology). While there can be no doubt that among some of the young laity and some of the young clergy there is closer and warmer communication than ever before, I am not absolutely confident that this warmth will be powerful enough to overcome the many negative factors to be observed in lay/clerical relationships.

What is absolutely imperative is that channels of communication between clergy and laity and between laity and hierarchy be opened as quickly as possible. The Vatican Council called for communication through the institutions that the Church has established for such purposes, obviously implying that the institutions ought to be established. But thus far in the American Church few such institutions actually exist, and until they exist and are functioning well, it would be my judgment that there would be nothing to prevent a constant rise in the level of anti-clericalism.

The problem of institutions of communication is closely connected with the somewhat larger question of the implementation of the Vatican Council. The Council stirred up a tremendous amount of hope, excitement, and expectation among clergy and laity alike, but unfortunately a good number of American Catholics feel that all the excitement of the Council was in vain and that there has been little or no change in the grass-roots life of the Church because of the Council. Indeed, time after time during our tour of American Catholicism in the past year I heard complaints about what respondents considered to be the frustration of the Council in the American

Church. As one middle-aged cleric pointed out to me, "It was much ado about nothing. I was tricked into believing something was going to change, but it hasn't. The same old shell game it always was."

It could be argued, of course, that the Council ended less than a half decade ago and that American Catholics will have to be patient until the structures are established that will enable the American Church to make the Council a reality in its grass-roots life. But, as a close observer of the social trends in the American Church, I am forced to report that neither the laity nor the clergy are placated by admonitions to patience. They want implementation, and they want it now. Such an attitude may be unreasonable, but it is a fact, and it is a fact with which the leadership of the American Church must deal. Five years ago I would have said that broad implementation of the Council would be satisfactory if it had occurred within five years after the conclusion of the Council, but now I am afraid that I am forced to conclude that we had far less time, and indeed it may already be too late.

By "too late" I do not mean that there is going to be massive defection from the Church, but rather that we are faced with the possibility of massive alienation from the organized Church. There is a myth abroad in the land that the Vatican Council has somehow or other done away with the need for ecclesiastical institutions and that Catholicism is indeed an institutionless community. Such a notion is, I believe, theologically incorrect, and is also a sociological contradiction. But neither theology nor sociology is going to shake it from peoples' minds, and the conviction that institutionalized Catholicism is incapable of reforming itself is becoming increasingly popular, especially among the younger and better-educated laity. These people will not leave the Church, but they will simply lose interest in its organized manifestations. They will consider themselves Catholics and practice their religion, at least according to their own lights, but will refuse to take seriously anything that the institutional Church says or does. In the short run, such alienation will not mean apostasy, but in the long run, over generations, it could very well mean a devitalization and atrophying of the Catholic community and eventually religious indifference, and then apostasy. Those responsible for decision making in the Church must face the fact that their decisions in the next couple of years are of critical importance because they can create problems with which the Church will have to wrestle literally for centuries to come.

Most of the problems I have just recounted would probably have existed even if American Catholicism were not socially mobile, even if the number of educated, economically successful laity were not rapidly increasing. My point is not that social mobility has generated these problems, but rather that it has aggravated them. It has made the need for solutions more urgent, the possibilities for dramatic change either of growth or decline more overpowering. For a social institution such as the American Church to handle two major transitions simultaneously is an awesome task, and those in leadership positions have every reason to be frightened by their responsibilities.

I have deliberately chosen in this presentation to emphasize negative possibilities in the adolescence of American Catholicism. The tremendous potential for self-destruction also involves tremendous potential for growth. It hardly needs to be pointed out that a rapidly mobile laity makes available a great pool of talent, energy, imagination, ingenuity, and dedication, but my purpose is not to congratulate American Catholicism on the brilliance of the present moment. I mean to talk about the possibilities of disaster, which are every bit as real as the possibilities for a new Golden Age. Neither growth nor decline is inevitable. What the American Church makes of the possibilities of the dual transitions of the present moment is subject to the free decision of men. Social mobility can be a curse or it can be a great blessing; it is up to us in the American Church to decide which it is going to be. I vacillate between optimism and pessimism, and will not in this presentation essay any guesses as to what the ultimate outcome will in fact be. But I shall conclude by observing that it is very late; indeed, much later, I fear, than most of our decision makers realize.

10. After Secularity: A *Post-Christian Postscript*

I intend to make three principal points in this chapter. The first is that the Catholic Church as it moves from the post-Tridentine Counter Reformation stance to the post-Vatican ecumenical stance is going through the same transition that the whole of Western society has undergone since the beginning of the nineteenth century —a change from Gemeinschaft to Gesellschaft.[1]

Secondly, I will contend that among the other contributions he makes to mankind, the Catholic sociologist can provide both the theory and the research to make this transition more fruitful for the Church of Rome, and can at the very same time, through his studies of the Catholic Church in transition, contribute a not inconsiderable increment to more-general sociological understanding.

[1] In a Gemeinschaft society, relationships tend to be few in number, intimate in quality, traditional in style, lifelong in duration, and strong in supportive potential. In Gesellschaft societies, on the other hand, relationships are multiple, transient, formless, and with only minimum supportive potential. In the former we relate with our total selfhood (however limited that may be), and in the latter most of our relationships involve only segments of our personality. (The classic example of the Gesellschaft relationship is that between the bus driver and his rider.) If one compares the peasant village from which one's ancestors came to Los Angeles, one has some idea of the poles of the Gemeinschaft-Gesellschaft continuum.

Thirdly, I would further contend that just as the Catholic Church is getting something of a late start in its transition into the modern world, it will travel the pilgrimage from Gemeinschaft to Gesellschaft much more quickly than did the rest of Western society. So, too, it will tend to evolve more quickly those post-Gesellschaft institutions by which modern secular man strives to maintain some of the advantages and supports of Gemeinschaft society in a Gesellschaft world. It will be of great interest both to the Church itself and to the rest of the human race to see what new forms of fellowship and community are evolved by the Catholic Church as it proceeds into the postsecular age, the age after the post-Christian age.

I have argued elsewhere that the real difference between Los Angeles and Ballendrehid (my ancestral home) is not that there is no Gemeinschaft in the former. Quite the contrary, there is probably more Gemeinschaft for most people in Southern California (excluding the phony variety at the "Institute"). The main difference is a fantastic increase in the sheer number of relationships, with most of the additional ones being very much of the Gesellschaft variety. The problem for the Angeleno is not that he experiences less support than he would have in Ballendrehid. He probably experiences more. In all probability, his relationship with his wife is much better than it would have been in the old country (but he and she expect far more than they would have in the old country). The problem is that he must shift constantly from a world of intimacy to a world of contractual and competitive formality. In addition, it may well be that unless the larger network of social relationships can be permeated by more Gemeinschaft, the smog will get worse.

My first proposition. The Catholic Church is becoming secularized —secularized not in the sense of secularism as it was condemned repeatedly by the American bishops, but rather secularized in Harvey Cox's sense of the word. From the point of view of the sociologist, the Vatican Council represents the Church's definitive break with the styles and patterns of behavior of a feudal and Renaissance world, and its assumption of the styles and patterns of behavior of the modern world. It should be made clear from the beginning that one can make the statement without necessarily implying that the modern styles are better than the feudal styles, that, rather, one can be content with simply saying that the patterns of the age of the post-Vatican Church are simply more appropriate for the Church in its work in contemporary society. In becoming secular it is putting aside the static, tribal, highly symbolic, ritualistic relationships that with some minor changes have been typical of it for half a millenium, and it is taking on the dynamic, rationalized, flexible, and technological relationships of the contemporary world. Just as the organization of the Church in the Middle Ages reflected the styles of organization to be found in the secular society (or perhaps vice versa), so the Catholic Church in the modern world can be presumed to take on the organizational style that is characteristic of any large corporate body in the modern world.

In short, the Catholic Church is on a pilgrimage from one end of the continuum of the Parsonian pattern variables to the other. It is moving from particularism to universalism, from ascription to achievement, and from diffuse to specific relationships. The Church is moving from familialism to professionalism, from paternalism to collegiality, and from feudalism to functionalism. It would perhaps be wise, in passing at least, to define these terms. By a feudal society I mean that style of behavior in which one man relates to the other with the totality of his person and belongs to the other in every element of his life. In a functional society, one man's relationship to another is limited entirely to a specific social function for which the relationship has come into being, and, when this function is not being fulfilled, then the relationship either changes completely or ceases to exist. Thus, an employer has authority over his employee in a functional society merely insofar as it contributes to the production of the particular goods or services for which they have come together. When they meet on the golf course, for example, the employer has no rights or prerogatives vis à vis his employee (save in feudalistic organizations such as the military). In a feudal society, a given type of behavior becomes virtuous if it contributes to the perfection of the relationship between a superior and a subject. Thus, for example, the virtues of poverty, chastity, and obedience are taken to be good because they symbolize the subordination of one man to another or of a group of men to God. In a functional society, on the other hand, these virtues are taken to be good simply because they contribute to the particular goals that have brought a group of men together, and are taken to have no particular value in themselves save insofar as they contribute to these specific sets of goals.

A classic example, one would suppose, is the relationship between pastor and curate. At the present time, the relationship is familialistic, paternalistic, and feudal. The curate is assigned not specific tasks or even to a specific parish; he is assigned to a specific man. This man is assumed, at least in theory, to be the only one who is capable of making a decision, and one who by his wisdom and experience is constituted a teacher and regulator of the curate in all his behavior. He is the father of the family, his power is absolute, his word is law, and the curate engages in only that kind of behavior that is specified and authorized by his feudal superior. Further, the pastor is assumed to have responsibility over almost the totality of the curate's life, to determine at what hours he may leave the parish house and return to it, whom he may see in his office, whom he may speak to on the telephone, how he spends his day off, when he takes his vacation, indeed virtually everything he does.

Such patterns of behavior are rapidly becoming obsolete. In years to come the priests who work together will be independent professionals, men highly skilled in their work who will come together to share the responsibilities of a particular mission, with one of their number perhaps acting as a chairman or as a senior colleague but only with highly limited and specified authority over the others and the right to give instructions only after some kind of consensus has been realized. The authority that the senior colleague has and the extent of relationships among colleagues will be determined purely by the nature of the work at hand and not by any ideal principles on how a subject and a superior should relate to each other. At that point, when the relationship among priests has become factual, professional, and highly specified, it will be able to be said that the relationship is no longer feudal or tribal, but secularized.

In the secularized Church, or the post-tribal Church, the same pattern of relationships will be presumed to exist among religious superiors and the other members of the community, between bishops and their priests, between priests and people, and between pope and bishops. Let us make no mistake about it: there will be many among us who will view this secularized Church as being somehow or other un-Christian, since they will have identified the transitory feudal forms in which the relationships among Christians have taken place for the past millenium with the essence of Christianity. Make no mistake about it further: there are a good number of the traditionalists among us who did not realize that the Vatican Council and particularly its affirmation of the principle of collegiality involved such changes. Yet, on the other hand, those of us who have studied human society and understand the inevitability of the shift from Gemeinschaft to Gesellschaft will realize that the traditionalists, those who resist the emergence of a postfeudal Church, are fighting their last, desperate rear-guard action.

It should be noted also that this transition from Gemeinschaft to Gesellschaft is accentuated in American society because, at the same time, the American Church is moving from the immigrant ghetto to the suburbs. The whole nature of this peculiarly American transition can be summed up by two propositions: First of all, about half of adult American Catholics are either immigrants or the children of immigrants, and secondly, American Catholics are every bit as likely to graduate from college and to go on to graduate school as American Protestants, and the average income of Catholics under forty is slightly higher than the average income of Protestants in the same age bracket even when the size of city and region of country are controlled. American Catholicism, now a full if still junior partner in the American experiment, stands with one foot in the old neighborhood in the central city and the other foot in the college-educated suburb. The results of this somewhat ambivalent situation are not surprising to the Catholic sociologists. We would cheerfully predict, even if empirical data were not all around us, that this would be a time of great fluidity in the American Church, of inevitable friction, of potentially revolutionary situations—a time of fashions and fads, of mercurial movements, of great hopes and rapid disillusions, of superficiality and divisiveness, of clericalism and anti-clericalism, of laicism and anti-laicism. It will be a time when, in the absence of profound and mature scholarship, our theories will be served up to us by journalists, and our controversies will tend often to be non-controversies in which serious questions such as clerical celibacy or Catholic education will be solved in the Catholic press mainly on the basis of what "I and my friends" happen to think now.

Nor will it be hard for the sociologists to prescribe what is desperately needed by a Church caught in the intersection of two transitions—Gemeinschaft to Gesellschaft and ghetto to suburbia. American Catholicism needs much more self-consciousness than ever in the past. It needs to understand who and what it is, where it has come from, and where it is going. It seems to me that American Catholicism has moved much further toward the flexible, experimental, rationalized Gesellschaft church than has Catholicism anywhere else in the world. We have understood, through our own experience for more than a century, what it means to be a church in an open society. Unfortunately, while our practice has often been the practice of a church in an open society, our theory, our rationalizations, our justifications, and sometimes our internal organization have been based on the ideology of the past, an ideology that not only has no relevance to what we have done in practice in the present, but has often been a handicap to us both in executing our authentic insights and in understanding the good we have done.

An astonishing example of this, I think, can be found in a school called Carroll College, in Helena, Montana. Carroll has the only seminary at a coeducational institution I know in the world, in which the divinity students and the predivinity students are integrated completely into the student body, save only that they do not date the coeds at the school. They live in the same residence hall, play on the same athletic teams, sing in the same choruses, perform in the same plays, go to the same classes, play cards in the same student union, and eat in the same dining room with the other students at the college. The traditional theory of Catholic seminaries would say that priestly vocations would hardly survive in such a worldly and secular atmosphere. It would be most unlikely, according to the theory, that some of the vocations could be developed in a situation in which young women were physically present with the seminarians for most of the waking day.

But the truth about the seminary at Carroll College is that it is, as far as I know, the only seminary in the country with a negative defection rate, which has more seminarians at graduation time than it did in the first year of college. Furthermore, well over three quarters of the Carroll seminarians persevere in their vocations through theology, and defections after ordination are apparently almost nonexistent. Finally, if one talks to the young people at Carroll College, seminarians and non-seminarians, young men and young women, one can find a profound and mature understanding of the priestly and lay vocations as well as the meaning of the celibate state. While the seminarians will laughingly say that the reason more young men enter the seminary than leave it through the college years is the absence of good-looking girls on the Carroll campus, I am prepared to say, from very limited and biased observation, that such an accusation is calumny. I would suggest, rather, that the seminarians are a far more important influence on the campus than anyone else, and because they are so attractive and so admired, many of the non-seminarians have a much greater insight into what the priestly life means and find themselves attracted toward the priestly vocation.

The seminary at coed Carroll College emerged for sheerly practical reasons: The Helena Diocese could not sustain a separate college and seminary, and then as time went on, the admission of coeds became a financial necessity. Despite all the theories that said it shouldn't work, it worked admirably well, but only now, after years of soft-pedaling the Carroll experience, has it begun to dawn on people that perhaps the pragmatic American instinct has discovered something about training young men for the priesthood and young

men and women for the lay state in contemporary American society
that is profoundly important, and not only for the United States but
for the whole Catholic world. It could just be that in a society such
as the United States, in a time such as ours, the best way to train
the people for the priesthood is to keep them as close as possible to
young men and women of their own generation who constitute the
Catholic laity of the future, and it could just be that this is the best
possible way not only for the future clergy, but also for the future
laity. It could be that the whole world can look at Carroll College
for a profoundly new and important understanding of the meaning
of growing up as a Catholic and growing up as a celibate Catholic.

Our increasing self-consciousness and our increasing understanding of what the American Catholic experience has meant will make
us much more confident of our own insights, much more secure as
we proceed to the development of ecclesiastical styles pertinent to
the American environment, and much more positive as we point to
the American way as most appropriate for the whole Church in the
modern world. Just as the American bishops and American theologians such as John Courtney Murray seem to have taught the rest
of the Church the meaning of religious freedom at the Vatican
Council, it could be that there are many more elements of the American way that could be of immense help to the rest of the Church.
In any event, the transitions we are in will certainly be rough and
rocky until we become much more self-conscious about who we are
and what we are doing.

To my second proposition. It should be perfectly clear that the
sociologists whose overriding theoretical concern for decades has
been the change from Gemeinschaft to Gesellschaft should be of
great help to the American Church in this time of transition. To
those who are impatient for more-rapid change and fearful that the
present change may be aborted, sociologists can say that transition
is inevitable once it has begun, as is the setting of the sun once it
has risen. To the open-minded traditionalist, sociologists can point
out that the transition through which we are now going need not
mean the end of the old values in the Church, but merely their

transformation into more-relevant values in the contemporary world. To the disturbed decision maker who doesn't know quite how to behave in the awkward times in which he finds himself burdened with responsibility, the sociologist can offer explanations derived from the experience of other institutions and the whole of society during the journey from one end of the Parsonian continuum to the other. To the Church, looking for new structures in which to institutionalize new patterns of behavior, the sociologist can propose serious research and experiments that will ease the transition and make it a more fruitful one. To American Catholicism seeking to understand itself, the sociologist can offer his tools for analysis and explanation.

It is lamentable that the institutional Church and the sociologist have not been engaged in dialogue nearly to the extent that they might. There has been much less done in the sociology of American Catholicism than one could have reasonably expected at this point in the development of sociology. Nor have the decision makers turned to the sociologists for advice and research nearly to the extent that they might have. The last lingering suspicions of the behavioral sciences have not yet completely disappeared from the land, and, as far as I am aware, not a single American Catholic sociologist was a consultant at the Second Vatican Council. I think I can make this observation with some grace, since when the Council was being organized I was not a sociologist and hardly a candidate for the role of peritus. There were of course sociologists at the Council, most of them European, most of them not nearly as well trained as their American counterparts. It may be chauvinistic on my part to observe that I think that both the Church universal and the American hierarchy would have been much better served if at least some of the sociological advice offered at the Vatican Council had been proffered by members of the American Catholic Sociological Society. But the past is the past and there is no point in lamenting it at great length. Nor is there any point, at least on this occasion, in trying to analyze the reasons for the wariness between the Catholic sociological fraternity and ecclesiastical administrators; whatever the past was, there are surely more than enough hopeful signs for us to conclude that the wariness is over.

But what is to be said of those who somehow or other feel that it is narrow and provincial for Catholic sociologists to be interested in the study of the Catholic Church? What is to be said to those who contend that the Catholic sociologist who concerns himself with the sociology of Catholicism is living in a ghetto world? One would have thought that Everett Hughes had answered that charge long ago when he wrote, "Nearly everything sociologically speaking has happened in and to the Roman Catholic Church." As non-Catholic sociologists become increasingly fascinated by the vast variety of sociological phenomena that are to be observed within the Church of Rome, it ill-behooves Catholic sociologists to pretend that when they study their own Church they become incapable of making a contribution to the broader concerns of sociological theory. Indeed, where else in the world can one find such a magnificent laboratory to study the transition from Gemeinschaft to Gesellschaft?

But Gesellschaft society is not like the Marxist classless society— the end-all and be-all of the evolutionary process. If anything is clear to sociologists at this stage of the game (though it does not at all seem to be clear to the theologians who read the more popularized sociological books), it is that Gemeinschaft has not died, that the family group, the ethnic community, the extended family, the religious denominations, are still terribly important pillars in the social structure. Indeed, it has become clear that if we so rationalize and formalize the social structure that a man's old, intimate primary-group relationships seem to be taken away from him, he will then proceed to build new primary groups for himself whether it be in the factory, the neighborhood community, the law office, the military establishment, or even the church. Anonymous man, in the face of the lonely crowd, living in miserable (or if you are a disciple of the younger Harvey Cox, splendid) isolation in a rationalized, formalized, mechanized, technological world is largely a figment of the sociological and, more recently, the theological imagination. Modern man, as we know him from our research experience (often opposed to our theoretical speculation) still wants all the Gemeinschaft he can find, be it in the extended family, the informal group on the job, or the religio-ethnic community that shields him from the impersonality of the larger society. It would be a mistake to feel that modern man wishes to return to the feudal. What he wants, rather, is to have the best of both possible worlds. He wishes to enjoy the warm, intimate support of Gemeinschaft at the same time he enjoys the freedom, the rationality, and the technological flexibility of a Gesellschaft world. Modern man wants to put aside irrelevant myths and the obsolescent sacred symbols of the past, but only so he might devise relevant and exciting new sacred symbols. Modern man wishes to put aside the primary groups in which his grandfathers were imprisoned and replace them with primary groups that enable him to enjoy even greater personal development and freedom. Modern man wants Community in the midst of his Associations. Modern man, in short, wants to be able to establish by free contract a new clan, a new tribe.

The surest sign of this hunger for new Gemeinschaft in the post-secular world is the tremendous vigor of personalism in contemporary America. The modern American is convinced that his happiness will emerge essentially out of human relationships, and if the modern American is young what he wants is "deep and meaningful relationships." Indeed, the modern young American, as fantastic an offspring of a marriage between Gemeinschaft and Gesellschaft as the mind of man could imagine, wants even to establish a deep and meaningful relationship with the bus driver. As a matter of fact, I someday expect to see the new breed arrive with picket sign in front of the bus terminal announcing, "We love the bus driver; why doesn't he love us?"

The personalist revolution is revolt against the detribalized society. It is a desire to establish once again in the human community the bonds of what Edward Shils calls "primordial ties," bonds that at least at one time were furnished by such things as blood, land, soil. If there is any primordial relationship that serves the same purposes today and that may eventually replace all the other primordial relationships, it is that of friendship. Indeed, to those of us who put aside our theoretical blinkers and take a hard empirical look at the modern world, the question is no longer whether the primary group will survive, but exactly what kind of primary groups will result from man's desperate longing for community. For it seems to me to still be in doubt that the postsecular community will rather replace the oppression and tyranny of the old Gemeinschaft society with a more subtle and more sophisticated neo-Gemeinschaft society.

For the Catholic Church, the question is the same. Will the old unfreedom of irrelevant, feudalistic forms be replaced by an authentic and free fellowship of the people of God, or is it to be approached instead by a new form of unfreedom, all the worse because it is described in terms of personalist philosophy and reinforced by all the subtle methods of manipulation that modern social psychology has revealed to us? Have we learned in fact that brainwash is brainwash whether you call it brainwash or whether you call it participatory democracy or a cursillo? Have we learned that tyranny is tyranny even if it is called freedom? Have we learned that men can be quite convinced they are free even though they are in fact subtly manipulated slaves? It is by no means clear whether the new fellowship within the Church, the new community of which I have written elsewhere, will destroy or reinforce freedom. It is by no means clear that the more intimate personalist groups that seem to be emerging all over the country will turn in upon themselves and rigidly restrict the freedom of their members or whether they will turn out on the rest of the world in a burst of love and trust and enthusiasm that could mark one of the great milestones in the development of human society. As the Catholic Church completes its transition from Gemeinschaft to Gesellschaft, there will emerge inevitably within it the small, subparochial or transparochial fellowships of believers that will give new depth and meaning to the collegial and functional Church resulting from the Vatican Council. Whether the new functional Church really is able to appeal to the profound longings in the heart of modern man depends on the success or the failure of these informal communities and fellowships of believers.

If we can say that, phenomenologically, original sin leads to the tragic inability on the part of man to love and to trust his fellow man, then we could affirm that the theological and philosophical personalism of our time, coupled with sophisticated social and psychological insights into the nature of human behavior, have made it possible for contemporary man to make a major and significant leap forward toward a more loving and more humanly fulfilling society.

If contemporary sociology and psychology (as well as theology, literature, and philosophy) have accomplished anything, they have taught us a much more profound understanding of the meaning of human relationships and how a community at the same time free and intimate, flexible and yet bound together by powerful forces, providing strong emotional support and yet open-ended, can be constructed. Unfortunately, misunderstood and inadequately understood group dynamics can readily turn what might have been a promising and free new community into a subtle form of tyranny. If Catholic sociologists and social psychologists cannot engage in intensive study of the new communities that are emerging, and if they do not provide meaningful generalizations as to crucial differences between free communities and tyrannies masquerading under the name of freedom, then the responsibility they must bear for this failure will be great indeed.

It would be my conclusion that historians of the future will look back at our time—the post-post-Christian world and the post-secularist society—as an era when man, at least Western man, had acquired freedom and abundance by leaving behind the Gemeinschaft world and moving into the technological Gesellschaft world, and then determined that it was humanly and psychologically possible to have the best of both, to combine the freedom and affluence of a technological society with the warmth and fellowship of a tribal society. Of course, whether historians of the future will also say that modern man, while he knew from social science that such community was possible, actually only discovered it in practice when the Roman Catholic Church, a relative newcomer in the pilgrimage to the Gesellschaft, was able to produce its own free human fellowships in the midst of a functional and secularized church, still is unclear. But if the historian of the future is able to make such an affirmation, then at least in one of his footnotes it seems to me that he will have to concede that a small, albeit important, part in this great leap forward toward the omega point was made by the Catholic sociologists who combined a sophisticated understanding of the dynamics of human society with a faith that at least in Christ Jesus modern or secular man is capable of loving.

11. Religion on the Catholic Campus

As a punishment for my sins I was required (by the Carnegie Corporation) to wander like some sociological Flying Dutchman around Catholic campuses, trying to understand the problems and prospects of Catholic higher education. A full account of the adventures my colleagues and I experienced on this hazardous journey will have to wait for another occasion. But one point at least needs to be made: it is now time for a serious consideration of the place of religion (as distinct from theology) on the Catholic campus.

The subject is an emotionally charged one, and it is very difficult not to be misunderstood. With some lack of confidence that I will be successful, let me try to establish the perspective from which I see the problem.

First of all, I view the purpose of the university (and the college) to be essentially intellectual; higher-educational institutions exist to pass on an intellectual tradition and to push back its frontiers. A Catholic university *as a university* has the same goals as any other university, but it adds theology to the intellectual tradition it wishes to hand on and to explore. A university, Catholic or otherwise, does not exist for moral training, for the inculcation of virtue, or for the indoctrination of spiritual values. It does not exist for these purposes not because it is ideologically opposed to them, but because by its very nature as a university it does not have the ability to accomplish such ends. If morality, virtue, and values have not developed in the context of previous institutions—home, neighborhood, parish, elementary and secondary school—then there is precious little that a university *as a university* can do about them; it is simply too late in the game, and any attempts a university as such may make to do remedial work in the value area simply is not going to be successful, because the university cannot do that for which it is not designed. The university by definition is designed for intellectual, not moral, goals; moral values are formed in infancy and childhood, or, short of special intervention of divine grace, they are not formed at all.

It is perfectly true that the university, through its presentation of scientific theology (and perhaps philosophy), can indirectly make a huge contribution to the development of a young person's value system; if he pays any attention to the questions raised in his theology class, he can engage in that re-evaluation of his childhood and adolescent religion that is necessary for it to become the religion of an adult. The theology learned in college can become the rational foundation for the faith of maturity, but the probability that this desirable goal will be achieved is in direct proportion to the scientific and academic excellence with which it is presented. If, for the slightest moment, it becomes moralizing or indoctrinating or pietistic or authoritarian, the young person will rebel against it, because he senses (and quite correctly, it seems to me) that a university course is being used for a goal not appropriate to it.

Secondly, since I believe that virtue is developed by the repetition of free human acts, I am opposed to compulsory spiritual exercises as part of Catholic university life, and am in favor of the maximum freedom commensurate with the common good of the university community. I cannot see how the notion that rules develop virtue can be harmonized with traditional Catholic theology or philosophy or with the practical experience of those who work with young people. Rules exist to maintain and preserve order, to protect the rights of individuals from encroachment by others, to promote an atmosphere of peace and harmony in which individual and collective development are possible, but rules don't make people virtuous. On the contrary, rules that attempt to compel virtue, in reality do more harm than good, because they readily turn people against the particular virtue they are forced to practice; thus, I am firmly persuaded that the compulsory retreat rule which still exists in all too many Catholic schools actually turns young people against retreats and does more harm than good to the spiritual life of many.

Finally, I think it is a mistake, and quite possibly dishonest, for Catholic educators to give the impression to parents that the morals of their children will be protected at Catholic colleges. In American society, at least, the morality of a young person can be protected in the final analysis only by the young person himself and by the convictions he has learned from his family. As one priest remarked to me, "If people want to sin around this school, there isn't much we can do to stop them, no matter how many rules we have." If parents have not done a good job of developing ethical convictions in their children, it is not safe to send them to any college. There may indeed be something in the community atmosphere of a Catholic college that will support values that already exist, but this support for values springs more from a consensus among the young people as to what is right and what is wrong (based on the convictions they already have) than on either the rules of the school or the theology taught in the classroom. The goal of education is of course the development of the whole man, but by the time the university is reached, about all that the formal educational institution can expect to affect directly is the intellectual development. The other aspects of the human personality system have already been shaped, for weal or woe.

I state these three assumptions not because they are particularly original nor because I wish to engage at the present time in a defense of them. Rather, I intend to use them as a framework for discussing the extremely important role that I think religion has to play on the Catholic campus. For, having apparently tossed religion out the front door of the Catholic college by insisting that all the college can hope to do is teach theology, I plan to bring it in the back door by pointing out that the university is also a community of Christians. Such an endeavor is more than an intellectual exercise; it seems to me that if we consider the various partners of the higher-educational enterprise to constitute a Christian community as described in the constitution on the Church, we will have a much clearer idea of what religion should be on the campus, and will be able to design a religious life for the campus that will help us to escape at least some of the dilemmas inherent in the question "Why have Catholic colleges?" The religion I hope to bring in the back door will not be tempted to use classroom lectures for indoctrination nor to impose virtue by rules, but it will make the Catholic campus the kind of Christian community that will add an extremely important dimension to the total experience of the young person who is part of it. As a university a Catholic institution of higher learning adds theology to the curriculum, but as a community of the people of God it provides a vital and exciting religious life for all those who belong to it. If the distinction between the two formalities is kept clear, the university as such will not take unto itself the role of religion, and the community of the faithful will not interfere with the work of the university. But the two institutions—university and community—will operate simultaneously in the same place and with the same people, though there may be considerable shifting of hats, depending on which formality is being emphasized. I am under no illusion that this distinction will solve all the practical problems of religion on the Catholic campus, but I do feel that it may provide a conceptual framework in which much fruitful discussion can occur.

Let us, then, begin. A Catholic campus is not only a locus for scientific and artistic instruction; it is also a place where a community of Christians have come together to enter into an established pattern of relations. It is a segment of the pilgrim people of God gathered together for a dialogue that is essentially intellectual. The intellectual dialogue may be only marginally affected by the fact that those engaged in it (faculty, administration, and students) are members of the pilgrim people. But by the very fact that they share communion with Christ through the Holy Spirit, their relationship will tend to transcend the merely intellectual and become one of Christian love; I say "transcend," not "replace" or "distort" or "substitute for." The loving relationship among the partners of the educational enterprise does not take the place of the most rigorous and professional kind of intellectual relationship; it does not in any way interfere with the intellectual relationship; it rather exists in addition to it. It may be stronger for some than for others; it may call forth greater commitment from one person than from another; it is essentially voluntary and not at all an academic requirement; it is rather the spontaneous outpouring of the inevitable love that results when two Christian persons encounter one another. While the Christian community on campus may take particular forms because some of those who belong to the loving community are young and others are older, it is in its essentials no different from any Christian community; and while the fact that there is serious intellectual concern in the campus community may give a certain tone to the love to be found in the campus community, many of the things to be said about this community could be said about any Christian community in which some members are a bit younger and others are a bit older.

In this chapter I wish to concentrate on the relationships between the young and the old in the loving community which is the campus. I will leave aside for another time the question of the implications of the constitution on the Church (not to say the encyclical *Quadragesimo Anno*) for relationships between faculty and administration and between clergy and laity in the campus Christian community. It suffices to say that we need not fear that there is no room left for improvement in these relationships.

If the Mass is the central event of the Christian life, summarizing symbolically the essence of our religious commitment, the most important element in any Christian community is its worship. Indeed, if the liturgy is not enacted with dignity and inspiration, then there is reason for grave doubt as to how Christian the rest of the life of the community will be. We must admit that we were singularly unimpressed with the campus liturgy in most of the schools we visited. The Mass is "available," which is to say that it is offered frequently and usually hastily, with the bare minimum of changes authorized by the constitution on the liturgy. But we came away with the impression that, in many of the members of the religious communities that administer the colleges, there is a notable lack of enthusiasm and even of understanding for the new liturgy, coupled with a regret that the old compulsory Mass-attendance rule became so unpopular that it had to be dropped. Often, it seems that the liturgical revival on campus consists essentially of having noon and evening masses and turning the altar around. Further, restrictions imposed by some chancery offices make it difficult in certain colleges to do even those things permitted by the constitution on the liturgy and by the American bishops; it would be hoped that diocesan officials would come to see that the campus community is a special one and that, whatever restrictions may be deemed necessary elsewhere in the diocese, they ought to be reconsidered before being applied to the campus.

Finally, I would note that the campus liturgy, such as it is, seems to involve only students; rarely do faculty, lay or clerical, participate in community worship together with the students—save at the compulsory Mass of the Holy Spirit at the beginning of the school year. The paternalistic ethos is still strong among many Catholic educators. When one observes that campus liturgy leaves much to be desired, the reaction is that there ought to be periodic community masses to which everyone will be obliged to come. Religious compulsion simply does not belong on the campus. What is required is that divine worship become an exciting, meaningful, dynamic event in the life of the Christian community on campus; if this happens, then voluntary attendance will increase rapidly; if it does not happen, forced attendance will not obscure the community's failure at that which is most essential. It seems to me that a campus which on the one hand enforces an elaborate system of rules and insists on compulsory retreats and, on the other, has an insipid liturgy, really does not understand what the Catholic Church is all about.

A second element in the religious life of the Christian community on campus arises from the fact that a large number of the members of the community are going through the process of developing child-

ish or adolescent religious faith into the faith of an adult. Christian
charity would demand that the community provide an atmosphere
in which this growth can most readily take place. Young people
should be free to talk about their religious problems (which, let it
be emphasized, are not "theological doubts" in the sense used in
the old moral-theology textbooks), their quest for meaning in life,
their anxieties about their own identity, the implications of their
religious belief for daily conduct. There are various ways in which
this can be done, but one method is the permissive, free-wheeling,
unstructured discussion group, presided over by a faculty member
and composed of those students who freely attach themselves to a
given faculty member for the purpose of discussing the meaning of
the Christian life. (It should be noted that discussion groups furnish
an excellent opportunity for "witness bearing" by lay faculty.) As
one who has participated in such groups for more years than I care
to remember, I can testify that they are wearying, frustrating, dis-
couraging, and probably the best, if not the only, way for young
people to translate the faith they have into practice and to grow
from childish faith to adult faith. There must not be a hint of indoctrination in these discussion groups, and they must be so interesting that young people will want to go to them. It is no solution to
argue that YCS and Sodality already serve this function; some few
groups surely do, but, by and large, the existing campus discussion
programs simply have not been dynamic enough to interest very
many young people; and to those who say that you cannot interest
young people in serious discussion of their religious commitments,
I offer as contrary evidence the Contemporary Problems Seminars at
Immaculate Heart College in Hollywood.

The paternalistic ethos listens to a discussion of the need for such
seminars, regrets that it is no longer possible to use the theology class
for these purposes, and immediately decides that a program of seminars is to be established to which students will be compelled to go.
The whole point has been missed: as soon as these discussion groups
become obligatory, they become worthless.

Thirdly, the Christian community which is the campus must be a place where young people can obtain help in solving the personal problems that, in our society, at least, beset those in late adolescence. It seems to be regrettably true that almost every upper-middle-class young person is going to need counseling at some point in his college years. The university is not in the counseling business; it exists to deal with the problems of the intellect, not of the emotions. But the Christian community must be profoundly concerned about the emotional sufferings of its members, for a young person with a serious problem is one of "the least of the brothers" and has a claim in charity on the help of the rest of the community. The formal counseling services at Catholic colleges are for the most part woefully inadequate, and need to be drastically improved. But formal counseling services are not enough, not nearly enough. The trouble with formal counseling is that it is "formal"; the young person must make appointments, fill out questionnaires, take personality tests, and admit that he is in need of a "head shrinker." (Furthermore, the contact with the counseling service of course goes on his "record," a record that, despite its confidentiality, has a way of coming into the possession of the FBI should the young person later be seeking security clearance.) Emotional problems are frequently pretty far gone before the young person is driven to seek formal counseling. Two additional types of counseling are needed: First, there must be available in much more informal circumstances a number of fully trained counselors who are not defined as "head shrinkers" but simply as people who are around and to whom you can talk when you need someone to talk to. For practical purposes, it would seem that most of these would be priests and religious. It is rather odd that we put priests and religious in dorms to maintain order and discipline, but do not put them there with the skills they need to listen sympathetically to the fears and anxieties of young people. But of course the paternalistic ethos is much more concerned with maintaining external order than practicing Christian charity. Secondly, in addition to those clergy and religious whose specific profession it is to be available to listen, almost all the religious functionaries on campus (and maybe some of the laity, too) should have enough training in psychology and enough charity so that they can spot a disturbed student when one approaches them, listen sympathetically, and help either by permitting the student to establish a relationship with them or by directing the student to someone who can help. It is harsh to say it, but most young people of college age are not persuaded that they are lovable (often because they have never been loved at home) and are desperately seeking love from the campus community. They haven't always been getting it.

This brings us to one of the most crucial elements of the religious life of the campus community of Christians: the clergy (and analogously the religious) must assume the roles of spiritual leadership in the community that the constitution on the Church insists is their function in the Church. On this subject there has been a great deal of nonsense spoken lately. We hear from younger religious that they are essentially academic professionals whose responsibility it is to bear witness to the Lord by excellence in their profession, and that personal involvement with their students is an obstacle to this academic excellence and must be kept at a minimum. (A dilemma that my colleague Peter Rossi has summed up as "publish or parish.") I often wonder who these religious faculty members are trying to kid. An academic skill does not absolve one from membership in the human race or in the people of God; nor does it remove the role of responsibility that comes from the clerical (and, to a lesser extent, the religious) state. Their research prevents them from becoming involved with people? Then their research is preventing them from being human beings. I would find this argument much more persuasive if the religious who use it showed any signs of awareness that the lay faculty is involved with its families to a much greater extent than the religious faculty is involved with students, and yet seems to get its research done. I do not think that the celibate state exists in the Church so that people can become productive research scholars; and if this is all that results from celibacy, the celibate scholar is very likely to end up a stale and crusty bachelor or spinster.

I presume that my own involvement in research gives me license to speak with some degree of conviction on the subject. It is not easy to combine pastoral work and research; it is presumably not easy to combine family life and research either; but it is not easy to be a human being, and we are not therefore authorized to take a simplistic way out by refusing to be human. Dr. Rossi's dilemma of "publish or parish" is one that cannot be resolved; to refuse to live with the dilemma is to refuse to love. We must do research, we must enter into loving relationships with those around us; some kind of lines must be drawn to prevent us from going to one extreme or the other, from so engaging in one role as to destroy the other. We will not have enough time until the day we die. If this is what the Christian life demands of us, then so be it.

If the Christian community on campus is a community of love, then we must expect that there will be great concern for the members of the community as persons. As a university, the campus may be content to view everyone as an IBM pack in the office of the registrar, but as a community of Christians, the campus must be deeply concerned about creating an atmosphere in which the quality of personal relationships can develop. The Catholic campus community is not worried about this problem because it fears that impersonality will lead to a Berkeley-like incident; it is worried because impersonality is un-Christian. Nor does it immediately become paternalistic and decide that we must have more compulsory "togetherness" to show that we who are members of the Zeta University "family" are all great friends. Rather, it strives to provide a climate in which spontaneous friendships can develop. It is very difficult to see how the gigantic dorms that are springing up on Catholic campuses can be very different in the social relationships they engender than their first cousins, the high-rise urban-renewal slums. The small dorms at Gonzaga, for example, and the small "college" approach being initiated in California at Santa Cruz, would seem to me to be particularly interesting innovations—especially if at Catholic schools these small units have a liturgical, apostolic, and intellectual life of their own.

It is very interesting, when one visits a large number of colleges in the course of a year, to note that the climate can be so very different in different schools. Some are warm, friendly, open places, while others are cold, tense, and unfriendly. The development of an authentically Christian atmosphere in the campus community is a matter for a book and not a few paragraphs in a chapter. But let no one say it cannot be done; two schools we visited, Barat College in Lake Forest, and Immaculate Heart in Hollywood, have been extraordinarily successful in this effort. The latter has a spirit of Christian "playfulness" unlike anything my colleagues and I have ever seen; we came away feeling that if the laughter that rings through the rather battered halls of IHC, and the charity and joy that radiate from the members of this Christian community, could be reproduced on, let us say, twenty Catholic campuses, there would be no question about the future of Catholic higher education—and probably no need for our research.

If the campus community is truly Christian, it will be engaged in dialogue within itself. Anyone who reads the campus newspapers at Catholic colleges is well aware that dialogue of a sort is going on. Unfortunately, it often seems that this dialogue is not real conversation, that neither the old nor the young are listening to each other. For the young there might be some excuse, because they are quite new to the skills of conversation; if at times they are unreasonable, if at times they shout, if at times it is difficult to know what they are trying to say, the reason is that they are young and are still learning how to converse. For the old there is less excuse. To shout back, to grow angry, to refuse to listen, to terminate the conversation by administrative fiat (by firing a newspaper editor, for example), to fail to engage in open discussion, constitute irrational behavior among those who are presumed to be adult. In addition, such behavior is at odds with what the constitution on the Church says about relations within the Christian community. But paternalism knows what is best for students, and need not engage in discussion. The paternalist is the boss, he makes the decisions; he is not interested in what the students say; if they don't like the way he runs his college, then they are perfectly free to go elsewhere. The only efficient way to run a college is to give commands and expect them to be obeyed; to let others share in the decision-making process is much too risky; it might lead to all kinds of disorder and confusion, and disorder and confusion are capital sins to the paternalist. And this is Christianity?

Finally, like all Christian communities, the campus community must not be closed in on itself; it must be engaged in the works of charity beyond its boundaries. Again, the picture varies from school to school: Some are deeply involved in the social problems of the larger communities of which they are a part, and others seem to be quite unaware that there are such things as social problems. In many instances, students are given very poor example by college administrators who with persistent myopia ignore the changing condition of the physical neighborhood in which the school is located. Many of the so-called apostolic activities of the so-called apostolic groups on campus are busywork. Yet the growth of the tutoring movement, for example, suggests that authentic apostolic energies are being generated in some campus communities. Nevertheless, I have often found myself wondering why CALM, one of the largest Catholic tutoring projects, did not grow out of a college atmosphere and has caused only perfunctory enthusiasm in some college communities. A closed community, it would seem, is no more happy with openness when it comes from the outside than when it arises from within.

The religious problems of the Christian community that is a college campus are quite clearly very complex, and in this chapter I have attempted only to begin discussion of a few of them. I must admit that I find myself quite overwhelmed by some of the other questions that might be raised: for example, in what sense is a commuter college a Christian community, and what role does a commuter student play in a community that also has residents? But because the questions are difficult and because there is still considerable room for improvement, it does not follow that we need despair. Catholic higher education is in an extraordinarily dynamic state at the present time, and it is not at all unreasonable to expect that just as the academic life of the campus community is improving, so the religious life can improve very rapidly. In my judgment two things are essential for such growth: First of all, religious life must not be confused with, or used as a substitute for, academic life. We cannot use the religious atmosphere of the campus as an excuse for inadequate academic standards, nor can we make religious functions part of the academic requirements. Secondly, it seems to me that the religious life of the campus community must be informal, voluntary, spontaneous, and open, if it is to have any vitality or appeal; a paternalism that attempts to indoctrinate morality and to compel virtue means death to the religious life of the campus.

Does the religious life of the Christian community that is the campus constitute a "Catholic dimension in higher education"? I think not. The Catholic dimension in higher education is theology. But I think that a vital religious community is a dimension of the life of Catholics who are engaged in the higher-educational enterprise. It is a dimension that cannot be neglected.

12. Sense and Sensitivity in the Catholic Church

The movie *Bob & Carol & Ted & Alice* is a devastating satire on encounter groups and pop psychotherapy. The four characters are cliché liberals who can use the jargon of therapy with a great deal of facility but little understanding. (Natalie Wood gives the clue to the nature of their liberalism when she says to Robert Culp—who incidentally looks a little lost without Bill Cosby—"We don't have any violence in this house; we don't even allow war toys.") After a marathon weekend at the "institute," Bob and Carol embark on an orgy of "honesty and openness," which soon engulfs Ted and Alice and leads eventually to a real orgy, in which both males discover that, despite their "deep insights" and "advanced viewpoints," they seem impotent when faced with the prospect of making love to each other's wife.

The shallowness and superficiality of the two couples led them to a denouement that was comic, or at least tragicomic. Not everyone who tries to play the therapy game is so lucky. One wonders whether the current romance between American Catholicism and group dynamics can lead to anything but tragedy. The "sensitivity" cult is a marvelous symbol of the superficial, shallow, anti-intellectual romanticism that presently besets the American Church and seems likely to cause religious impotence.

Make no mistake about it: Substantial segments of the elite groups in American Catholicism are hooked on an extraordinary collection of group experiences running all the way from the quite limited "orthodox" T-groups sponsored by the National Training Laboratories to the berserk nude marathon sessions of the Esalen variety. If one can explain the overwhelming popularity, not to say virtually unquestionable sanctity, of groupism to many Catholics, despite the fact that the theories behind such group experiences are questionable, the practical results dubious, and the dangers evident, one will have gone a long way toward explaining the present crisis in the American Catholic Church.

One must begin such an investigation with sensitivity training, both because it is the granddaddy of all groupism and because the orthodox sensitivity sessions of the NTL variety are the green wood of groupism. If one can raise serious questions about sensitivity training, the same questions are even more serious for the more-radical group gimmicks.

Edgar H. Schein and Warren G. Bennis are among the more restrained and moderate of the theoretical advocates of sensitivity training. For them the learning process in the T-group is essentially an educational experience. Those who have gone through such an experience emerge, ideally, with "an increased awareness of their own feelings and the feelings of others." They also become more aware of "the complexity of the communication process" and are more ready to accept the "genuine differences in others' needs, goals, and ways of approaching problems." They may also become more aware "of their own impact on others" and "of how groups function and the consequences of certain kinds of group actions." (Schein, E. H. and Bennis, W. G. *Personal and Organizational Change Through Group Methods: The Laboratory Approach.* New York: John Wiley & Sons, 1965.)

Louis A. Gottschalk describes how the learning experience is supposed to take place: Finding themselves in an unstructured situation in which the leader resolutely refuses to establish a structure for the group to operate in, "in their effort to supply structure where it is absent, group members vie with one another to propose a program of operation, an organization and rules of procedure. However, to do so, each group member falls back on his personal experiences of how groups should function, and each participant attempts to set up the organization of the group in a way that fits his experience, inadvertently attempting to reproduce in the T-group his typical role and function in other groups. Other group members are at the same time attempting to fill in the leadership gap and to set up their concept of group organization. In this competition there is a vying for leadership. Individual approaches which are proposed that do not take into consideration the individuality of each group member but rather tend to force the other members into a mold, stemming from one's previous private experiences in other, different groups, are met with opposition and challenge. The self-centered individual, the manipulator, the person who neglects to keep his fingers on the pulse of each individual in the group, the rebel for rebellion's sake, the peacemaker, the person who characteristically stays on the sidelines—all these personality types and others reveal themselves to the group. If they are attuned to the feedback available from other group members, they will be offered a reflection of themselves as they perform in their customary roles." (Gottschalk, L. A. "Psychoanalytic Notes on T-Groups at the Human Relations Laboratory, Bethel, Maine," *Comprehensive Psychiatry*, Dec. 1965, p. 472.)

A similar description of the process is given by Bradford and Gibb: "A T-group is a relatively unstructured group in which individuals participate as learners. The data for learning are not outside these individuals or remote from their immediate experience within the T-group. The data are the transactions among members, their own behavior in the group, as they struggle to create a productive and viable organization, a miniature society; and as they work to stimulate and support one another's learning within that society. Involving experiences are a necessary, but not the only condition of learning. T-group members must establish a process of inquiry in which data about their own behaviors are collected and analyzed simultaneously with the experience which generates the behaviors. Learnings thus achieved are tested and generalized for continuing use. Each individual may learn about his own motives, feelings, and strategies in dealing with other persons. He learns also of the reactions he produces in others as he interacts with them. From the confrontation of interventions and effects, he locates barriers to full and autonomous functioning in his relations with others. Out of these he develops new images of potentiality in himself and seeks help from others in converting potentialities into actualities." (Bradford, L. P., Gibb, J. R., and Benne, K. B. "Two Educational Innovations," in *T-Group Therapy and Laboratory Method*. New York: John Wiley & Sons, 1964.)

It would be difficult to take exception to the process he has described in the previous quotes, although one must admit that it's a long way from the sober pages of Schein and Bennis to the public orgasms described by Robert Blair Kaiser in a recent issue of *Playboy* or to the mad enthusiasm of some of the self-enlightened sensitivity prophets in American Catholicism. To learn how groups work, to understand one's own impact on others, to become aware of one's own emotions in group interactions, all these are surely praiseworthy goals. But the corruption of these goals into bizarre foolishness is not pure accident, for as Louis Gottschalk points out in his sensitive report on his own experiences at the National Training Laboratories in Bethel, Maine, there is apparently inherent in the T-group experience a process that is both dangerous and easily abused. Indeed, Gottschalk notes that in two of the groups he observed at Bethel, at least half of the participants had "obviously acute pathological emotional reactions." It is curious, as he observes, that an "educational process" in which participants are somewhat carefully selected and that is not, at least in the Bethel manifestation, described as therapy, still becomes psychologically disrupting.

After considering the process at great length, Gottschalk concludes that the T-group "somehow sets in motion reactions that also occur in the psychoanalytic situation." Indeed, according to Gottschalk, the T-group experience is essentially a "transference neurosis." The T-group leader's refusal to set a structure, the prelab propaganda, and

the evangelical promotion by ex-T-group members create a situation in which the participant is able to project and act out his needs
with regard to parents, his anxiety about conflicts, and his misper-
ceptions with respect to authority figures. In other words, the
T-group situation facilitates, encourages, and depends upon regression to childhood behavior patterns among its members. The leader
becomes a parent figure, and the other members sibling figures; and
the absence of structures creates a situation in which the normal
inhibitions that prevent us from acting out our transference neuroses
are removed.

The "trainer" refuses to set limits on either the speed of the appearance, or the intensity, of the transference reaction, since he be-
lieves as a matter of principle that the group will provide reality
checks for each other. Schein and Bennis are emphatic on this
point: "Most important in developing a culture of psychological
safety is the power of the T-group itself. For restoring equilibrium of
its members, for reducing threat, there is no substitute for the group.
We are always amazed at the supportive and ameliorative strength
of the group . . . the main source of psychological safety for the individual is his sense of support and strength earned in and somehow
borrowed from his T-group."

But Louis Gottschalk is more than a little skeptical about the re-
liability of the group as a reality check: "The flaw in this hope is that
other group members as well as the trainer are capable of these
transference-like reactions to the point that the expression of some
forbidden impulses is frequently met from some group members with
harshly repressive, condemning, rejecting responses . . . group members with high self-esteem and ego-strength survive the impact of . . .
exposing their irrational and rational selves and getting stepped on
or of observing and participating in the harsh limit setting of others.
These T-group members report enthusiastically about having a
growth or learning experience . . . insecure individuals are often se-
verely upset by the T-groups and in their shame, they say little about
their experiences."

Thus, the very process by which the T-group participant is supposed to become more aware of group interaction and his own impact on others is a regression to infantile behavior. As a matter of fact, at least one T-group theorist admits that anxiety is specifically caused by the absence of structure in order to produce "optimal regression." (Whitman, R. M., "Psychodynamic Principles Underlying T-Group Processes," in Bradford, L. P., Gibb, J. R., and Benne, K. B., *T-Group Therapy and Laboratory Methods.*)

As Jaffe and Scherl note, "The Situation is deliberately designed to lower defenses. In theory this occurs in the presence of reduced threat, which in turn permits learning to take place. In actuality . . . defenses may be lowered without compensating support of mechanisms becoming available." This raises the risk of psychopathological reactions occurring, and Gottschalk comments that frequently there is no reason for a participant to expect that he will in fact learn from the feedback process what impact he does have on others. "The reflection is usually distorted rather than clear and sharp, for the reflecting surface of these human mirrors is roughened and distorted by the perceiver's own opinions, values, and emotional conflicts." In other words, there is considerable reason to doubt that the group can be counted on to be either an effective reality check or an accurate mirror. If it fails in either or both of these respects, then the educational experience does in fact involve a regression to infantile behavior patterns. It can become very dangerous when the group is not able to play the corrective role that sensitivity theory expects of it.

One concludes, therefore, that the T-group process can fail or even become positively dangerous if the group is not presided over by a highly sophisticated leader and is not composed of reasonably mature, self-possessed human beings. With the proper selection of both leader and members, and proper safeguards, sensitivity training can, one assumes, be a useful learning experience for certain people. The recommendations of Jaffe and Scherl, as endorsed by the *Journal of the American Medical Association,* are extremely pertinent: "Participation must be voluntary and informed; participants must be screened. Thorough limits must be set regarding acceptable behavior and individual follow-up should be given." (Jaffe, S. L. and Scherl,

E. J., "Hazards of T-Groups," *Journal of the American Medical Association*, October 27, 1969, p. 719, quotes Jaffe, S. L. and Scherl, E. J., "Acute Psychosis Precipitated by T-Group Experiences," *Archives of General Psychiatry*, 1969, pp. 443–48.)

But many T-group trainers are willing to make a virtue out of necessity and to argue that the transference/regression process, which is the core of sensitivity training, ought to be encouraged and promoted rather than restrained. The more regression, the better, and sensitivity training becomes not merely a limited learning experience, but an emotional rebirth, a profound, enriching, and deeply moving emotional experience that transforms the participant, heightens his sense of awareness, and changes his whole life. Once one has determined that sensitivity training is not just an educational experience, but a dramatic psychological happening, once one has turned regression into an end in itself, one has begun the journey down the path from Bethel to the nude marathons of Esalen.

Trainers will disagree over whether sensitivity experience is psychotherapy or not. Those who see it as a limited educational experience in which one becomes aware of one's impact on others will deny that it is psychotherapy. Those who explicitly or implicitly view regression as an end in itself will either cheerfully admit that what they are engaging in is a therapeutic process or deny the relevance of the question, but their response does not matter. To induce transference neurosis and regression to infantile behavior patterns as a means of remaking the personality is very clearly to engage in psychotherapy, and psychotherapy of an intense variety. Group therapy is a fine thing, but it is far more than an educational experience, and those who practice it without proper clinical training and license should be called what they are—charlatans and quacks.

If psychological reactions are possible, even in the conservative and orthodox T-groups of Bethel, one can imagine the possibility of emotional harm in groups in which everything is done to maximize the regression, complete with singing, finger painting (each other), pawing, handling, pushing, shoving, caressing, screaming, ranting, raving, pounding—all, of course, preferably without any clothes on.

Such regression experiences are extraordinarily dangerous, even for the relatively stable. For the unstable they can be a disaster and, in some cases, have even led to suicide. But it is, of course, precisely the unstable who are attracted to such bizarre experiences in the first place. There is little justification in psychological theory for putting even a stable, healthy person through such an ordeal and absolutely no justification for doing it to someone who is less than stable. Twenty-four-hour therapy or two-week therapy can be validated neither by psychoanalytic theory nor by any proven empirical result. It is a dangerous, irresponsible, foolish practice, and the evangelical enthusiasm for it is not unlike the evangelical enthusiasm of the drug user. The reasons behind the enthusiasm are, one suspects, the same. The lonely, the frightened, the dispossessed, the troubled, the uncertain, the confused, need their kicks. Collective regression is the functional equivalent of rock music or drugs in the providing of kicks. Of course, one's awareness is heightened by such an experience, but such enlarged awareness is artificial, temporary, and far more likely to contribute to the bizarre aberrations of Bob and Carol when they return from the institute than it is to healthy, permanent personality growth. In other words, sensitivity training as a learning experience can be valuable under the proper circumstances, but involves certain risks. But massive transference and regression as instant therapy is not only dangerous, but insanely foolish.

As Martin Lakin has said recently, "More serious is the fact that there is little evidence on which to base a therapeutic effectiveness claim. To me it seems indefensible that advertising for training should be as seductive as it is in offering hope for in-depth changes of personality or solutions to marital problems in the light of present inadequate evidence that such changes or solutions do occur. . . . A legitimate case could perhaps be made for the temporary alleviation of loneliness that is unfortunately so widespread in contemporary urban and industrial life, but the training experience as a palliative is neither learning about group processes nor is it profound personal change." (Lakin, M. "Some Ethical Issues and Sensitivity Training," *American Psychologist*, Vol. 24, No. 10, October 1969, p. 925.)

The sensitivity cult as practiced in American Catholicism, one very much fears, often involves far more of the maximum regression as salvation event than it does a limited educational experience. Few of the Catholic "trainers" have had any kind of professional training, and most of them are far more interested in therapy and salvation than they are in limited learning. Screening of either leaders or members seems to be infrequent; participants are not only uninformed, but, in many cases, not even free not to attend. Seminarians, nuns, students, priests participate in sensitivity sessions not because they freely choose to, but because they have to, either at the command of their superiors or as a requirement for academic credit. One wonders why so many of the professional Catholic liberals are silent at this incredible abuse of human freedom.

The dramatic change created in the Church by the Vatican Council has destroyed many outmoded structures, but, in the process, we have become a church without theological or organizational context. Emphases on process and relationship are an excuse from the hard, difficult task of developing new intellectual visions and new organizational structures. Indeed, the Church seems to have become one gigantic T-group, with little structure, high levels of anxiety, and vast regressions to infantile behavior patterns.

We have also discovered or rediscovered, in the post-Conciliar era, our emotions; collective regression turns out to be a marvelous way of getting emotional "kicks" or going on emotional "highs" without either obligation or effort. We do not have to develop new convictions, make new commitments; we do not have to assume responsibility for our own behavior or for our relationships with others; we don't really have to do anything but "let go" and "feel good." Blowing our mind and going on emotional binges are marvelous substitutes for dealing rationally and civilly with problems in the real world.

The words of Gottschalk and Pattison are appropriate:

. . . Thus the T-group may foster a sense of pseudo-authenticity and pseudo-reality—that this is really living while the rest of life is phony. The reality of the situation may be that the T-group participant can afford to act in ways that ignore reality because he does not have to live with the consequences of his behavior. Some people return to national sensitivity groups year after year because, they feel, "here I can really be myself." They are in fact unable to be themselves. Or they may be inappropriately capable of sharing intimate details of their psychological experience in a group of people without being able to do so when they should with a single individual. (Gottschalk, L. A. and Pattison, E. M., "Psychiatric Perspectives on T-Groups and the Laboratory Movement: An Overview," *The American Journal of Psychiatry*, Vol. 126, No. 6, December 1969, p. 834.)

Our sexuality and our aggressiveness have been released and legitimated in the new Church, and there is a lot of pent-up aggression and sexuality left from the old Church. Regression situations allow us to release our aggressions and to indulge in sexually titillating behavior without having to face possible consequences for such actions. The relationship between man and woman, for example, in T-groups is, for all the absence of structure, highly ritualized and stylized. None of the constraints that reality imposes on ordinary human relationships apply in the emotionally charged atmosphere of group regression. The styles and the rituals of such an "anything goes" environment are not styles and rituals appropriate for everyday life—as many priests and nuns whose romances began in such situations discover very shortly after their wedding day.

Gottschalk and Pattison are quite devastating on the subject of the shallow selfishness that the "anything goes" atmosphere creates:

> The T-group may foster a concept that anything goes regardless of consequences. Instead of creating interpersonal awareness it may foster personal narcissism. If an individual says anything he wishes, then he may come to assume that just because he feels like expressing himself is justification enough to do so. This may preclude effective communication, for he then ignores whether the other person is receptive to his message, and he ignores the effect of his message on the other person. Communication may not be seen as an interpersonal event but merely as the opportunity to express oneself. The principle of "optimal communication" is ignored for the principle of "total communication." (p. 835.)

We cannot escape the rather harsh reality that a good many priests and religious were recruited as adolescents, trained in adolescent environments, and forced to behave as adolescents in rectory or community life. The passive-dependent personality was one over which it was easy to exercise social control in the pre-Conciliar Church. But the controls have collapsed, and these psychological adolescents now are faced with the need to have strong convictions, firm commitments, and a clear grasp on the reality of who they are. Unfortunately, they have a very low tolerance for ambiguity and complexity. They must obtain their identity overnight (even though psychological theory says this is quite impossible). Therapy, either individual or group therapy, takes too long, but a regression experience promises maturity and identity overnight—with little effort. That's just what an adolescent wants.

In addition, if one is willing to proclaim oneself an expert in sensitivity training, one can achieve competence without effort or training. Two weeks in Bethel, a weekend of T-grouping, or even twenty-four hours, and one has become a fully certified Messiah, ready to bring salvation to any group that is willing to ask for it or even willing to tolerate it when it is imposed upon them. For the priests or religious who are not sure what a priest or religious ought to be doing, to become a sensitivity Messiah is an extremely gratifying event. One can manipulate people, play games with their emotions, and act as a guru for them, all without risking oneself, assuming any responsibility, or acquiring any particular technical or scientific skills.

One self-trained therapist recently remarked during a television interview that the best judges of whether someone is qualified to act as a group leader are the group itself, a form of argumentation that is roughly analogous to maintaining that the best one to determine a brain surgeon's competencies is the patient on whom he is going to operate. In Lakin's words, "The fact that the consumer seeks or agrees to these experiences does not justify them as ethically defensible or psychologically sound. . . . It cannot be assumed that the participant really knows what he is letting himself in for." (p. 926.)

There are, in summary, three principal objections I have to sensitivity training:

1. It is a transference/regression phenomenon, theoretically a limited one caused for learning purposes; however, unless the leader is very skillful and the participants carefully chosen, the limitations are likely to slip away.

2. The faith of the sensitivity theorists in the ability of the group to serve as a reality check and an accurate reflection of how its members behave does not seem to be justified by clinical studies that have been made. Unless the conditions described in the previous paragraph obtain, the group cannot play either of these roles very well.

3. When unlimited regression is induced as an end in itself, or as a means to create a "profoundly moving" and regenerative personality experience, the process becomes an exercise in psychotherapy and a brutal and dangerous one at that. Most of those who preside over such experiences do not seem to have the knowledge, the training, the personal self-possession, or the license to engage in therapy.

The human personality is a delicate and complex system. One introduces a transference/regression process into this system only at considerable risk. It is no exaggeration to say that a regression experience is the psychological equivalent of major surgery. It is not to be undertaken lightly, nor unless there is a clearly demonstrated need, and always with careful safeguards, and under the direction of a well-trained professional. Those eager young priests who, with no training, no supervised internship, and no license, induce a transference/regression process in other human beings, are every bit as irresponsible as if they engaged in open-heart surgery. If the various priests' associations around the country can ever move beyond the needs of priests themselves and become concerned about the problems of the larger Church, it is to be hoped that they will set up ethical-practices committees that will protect the faithful from the activities of such quacks.

One of the more unfortunate results of the undisciplined craze for sensitivity training is that an important contribution of group dynamics is either ignored or tarred with the sensitivity brush. A trained psychologist can make a major contribution to a working group by helping the members of the group to understand their problems of communication and thus facilitating the efficiency and effectiveness of their work. In such an effort there is no attempt at causing regression, no effort to provide a "deeply moving experience," and surely no attempt to create "meaningful community." The psychologist's goal is much more modest: he merely wants to help a functioning community to function better. He must exercise restraint to turn back those who would like to see the community become a therapy group (so it could stop working) and must limit the time and extent of his activity. But he is likely to accomplish far more positive growth than all the sensitivity messiahs in the world.[1]

[1] Gottschalk, L. A. and Pattison, E. M., "Psychiatric Perspectives on T-Groups and the Laboratory Movement," p. 827. Gottschalk and Pattison distinguish between three types of laboratory groups: 1) the sensitivity, personal encounter, or T-group; 2) the task-oriented group involving structured group exercises aimed at teaching group-function skills; and 3) intervention laboratories that are established for functional work groups in the community or industry. The two authors seem to lament the fact that the latter two manifestations of the laboratory movement have become lost in the cult of personal growth through group experience. They go on to say (p. 837):

"To summarize the assets and liabilities of the T-group method, it may be stated that the T-group presents a powerful means of involving people in human behavioral analysis. The method provides possibilities for a highly significant contribution to the humane quality of existence in our culture and its various work and community components. The training laboratory has potential as a powerful instrument. Its liabilities lie in the area of utilization, as with any powerful instrument. Without adequate training, supervision, and guidelines, a powerful instrument may be destructive, just as a valuable drug may have undesirable effects if used unwisely or in incorrect doses. The liabilities described are not intrinsic deficits; rather, they are deficits of training, experience, clarity, and precision of goals. . . . They can be avoided. Leaders within the laboratory movement are addressing themselves to the task.

"Of more concern are the peripheral and derivative products of the laboratory movement groups that have picked up bits and pieces of the laboratory movement, without the democratic concerns of the originators, without the clinical experience of the early leaders, without even the informal communicative guidelines that tend to keep professionals within a self-corrective framework, and with-

Can sensitivity training accomplish anything worth while? There is some theoretical reason to believe that the original goals of the NTL type of sensitivity group—stated at the beginning of this chapter—can be achieved, although a recent review of the literature of the impact of sensitivity experiences on business executives is, at best, inconclusive on the subject of whether there is any impact at all. But there is no reason to think that group dynamics will provide instant therapy, instant identity, or much of anything else save emotional confusion and injury. If you have a strong personality and want to learn something more about your impact on others, a sensitivity group, provided it is presided over by a psychologically sophisticated and well-trained leader and is composed of carefully screened participants to whom both the nature of the experience and limitations on behavior are made clear will certainly do no harm and may be of some help. If, however, it is therapy you want, then seek it from an approved therapist, either in private sessions or in a legitimate therapy group. If you're looking for emotional kicks, jolts, and highs, then by all means seek out a regression group, preferably with a "trainer" who is an unsophisticated extrovert (the model provided by *Bob & Carol & Ted & Alice* will do splendidly). And you might just as well take off your clothes and start pawing the others in the group, because this is a proven way of expediting regression; never mind the remark of a psychiatrist who said, "If you have a neurotic take off his clothes, what you have is a nude neurotic."

If, on the other hand, you respect your own integrity and dignity, have nothing to do with the gospel of salvation through regression; if you are a religious or a priest or a seminarian and your superior attempts to force you into a sensitivity session, stand on your rights as a human being and a Christian and refuse. If they insist, then appeal to the local bishop of the appropriate Roman congregation.

---

out the continuing inquiring, self-critical, self-evaluative, and research perspective.

"It is perhaps paradoxical that despite the enthusiasm that the laboratory movement has fostered, its practitioners have not fully realized how powerful are the tools they have developed. Therefore, the enthusiasm may not yet be tempered by respect and concern that these tools be rightly used."

The Roman regulations on manifestation of conscience easily cover compulsory therapy or compulsory sensitivity training. If you are a student in a Catholic educational institution and are constrained to participate in a sensitivity group, appeal either to the bishop or to the American Association of University Professors, and if you are a plain Catholic layman and someone tries to disrupt your particular group with comments such as, "I hear you saying," or "I don't think you're being completely open and honest," or "I think there are some feelings here that we ought to get out into the open," then discreetly observe that the real problem may be that there is not enough insensitivity in the Church and that you may be willing to demonstrate how it is practiced.

13. The First Papal Press Conference: A Dream

(Kevin Cardinal Orsini was elected Pope by "inspiration" on the forty-third day of the conclave; ninety-six-year-old Cardinal Antonelli leaped from his throne in the Sistine Chapel and shouted in his feeble voice, "Orsini Papa!" With varying degrees of weariness, surprise, dismay, and joy, all the other cardinals echoed the shout: "Orsini Papa!" It was then pointed out by several of those present that this was indeed a legitimate and definitive way of selecting a pope, even though it was one that apparently had not been used in the history of the Papacy. Almost without realizing it, the cardinals had selected their youngest member, the forty-six-year-old Orsini, as the new Pope. There were some, later on, who claimed that Antonelli had been sound asleep, and in his sleep had had a nightmare of Orsini becoming Pope. His cry of "Orsini Papa!" it was alleged, was not an inspiration from the Holy Spirit, but the result of a bad dream. In any case, Orsini's supporters had seized the opportunity to proclaim their man the victor, and after forty-three days of a conclave in which nine cardinals had already died, no one was prepared to dispute his claim to the Papacy.)

In his first act as Pope, Orsini, now known as Kevin I, giving the traditional blessing, *Urbi et Orbi*, in a black business suit and tie, had announced that, while he had deep respect for the college of cardinals, and had every intention of continuing it as an important arm of the Church, he thought it would be inappropriate, under the circumstances of the modern world, to continue the college as the papal electoral body. He announced that henceforth the Pope would be elected by all the archbishops of the world. "Unless," he added, "my colleagues in the Synod can come up with a better idea."

The day after his election, Orsini announced the first English-language papal press conference. Before the Pontiff arrived in the banquet room of the Rome Hilton, where the conference was to take place, members of the Vatican press corps compared notes on the very strange background of Kevin I. His father was Prince Raffaele Orsini, now a member of the Italian Senate, and his mother Princess Annie (nee O'Brien) Orsini, a Dublin actress whom Prince Raffaele had wooed and wed while he was the third secretary of the Italian mission to Dublin. Their son had been raised in the Flatbush area of Brooklyn while Prince Raffaele was on the staff of the United Nations, and he had attended Fordham University and the Harvard Graduate School of Business before beginning his theological studies at the Pontifical Gregorian University. His rise in the papal diplomatic service had been meteoric, but his reputation for pragmatism, liberalism, and a somewhat off-beat sense of humor, as well as the fact that he spoke both Italian and English with a Brooklyn accent, had made him an unlikely candidate for the Papacy.

Kevin I, attired in a gray Savile Row suit, light blue shirt, and Paisley tie, finally arrived at the Monte Mario for his press conference, a transcript of which appeared the following day in the New York *Times:*

Q. (*Times* of London) Your Holiness, the whole world is wondering—

A. Please don't call me Your Holiness. I don't know that I'm all that holy and it's sort of an old-fashioned name. You can call me Pope or Mr. Pope, but please don't call me Your Holiness.

Q. Well, yes, sir. The whole world is wondering what your position
will be on the birth-control issue.

A. I think it's a very complex issue and one that I certainly
wouldn't want to address myself to in any specific detail this
morning. We have really messed up this sex business in the
Church for a long time and I don't think we're going to be able
to make any coherent Christian statement on family planning
until we do a lot of thinking and talking about the whole question of sexual personalism. I'm going to summon the Synod of
Bishops into session the week after next, and it's certainly going
to be one of the top items on my agenda to ask my colleagues
if they will set up a commission to consider a statement on the
meaning of sex in the Christian tradition.

Q. (Chicago *Sun-Times*) Do we understand, then, Mr. Pope, that
you intend to convene the Synod of Bishops at once?

A. Why, yes, of course I do. This is an extremely difficult job I've
been saddled with, and I certainly don't intend to try and do it
all myself. What's the point of having all these bishops through-
out the world unless they're going to bear some of the responsibility? I'm going to have them in session for a couple of months
every year for the rest of my administration, and they may as
well resign themselves to buying commuter tickets to Rome.

Q. (*Times* of London) But, sir, if I understand you correctly, there
is going to be some considerable delay before you address yourself to the birth-control issue. In the meantime, aren't you afraid
that most Catholic couples will continue to consider artificial
contraception a mortal sin?

A. No, I don't think so. If they do think it's a mortal sin, they are,
in my judgment, wrong, but I'm certainly not going to try and
impose my views on their conscience—at least not until I have
been advised by my colleague bishops.

Q. (St. Louis *Post-Dispatch*) There has been considerable talk of
restoring the practice of popular election of bishops to the Catholic Church. Would you care to comment on this possibility?

A. Oh, I'd be happy to comment. Two of my predecessors of happy memory—I can't quite remember what their names were, but they were back in the sixth century—said that it was sinful to choose a bishop by any other method besides popular election. Being at heart a very conservative fellow, I agree with them, so I'm going to do everything in my power to sell the Synod of Bishops on restoring popular election as soon as we can. It may take a bit of selling, but when they see how tough the job is going to be in my administration, I think a lot of them are going to be only too happy to have a successor in four or five years.

Q. (St. Louis *Post-Dispatch*) Then, am I to understand, sir, that you are in favor of limited terms for bishops and perhaps even for the Pope?

A. Well, if you think I'm going to stay in this office until I die in it, you're sadly mistaken. This may be a fine job for five or ten years, but after that I'm going to want to retire someplace where it's peaceful and quiet. It doesn't seem to me to be fair to ask anybody to hold a major leadership position for more than five, or ten, years at the most. I assume that when the Synod of Bishops ponder this matter at some length, they will agree with me.

Q. (New York *Times*) Have you made any decisions about the selection of a papal cabinet?

A. That's a very good question, Scotty, and I'm not sure that I can give a complete answer, but at least I have some ideas: Sister Mary Luke is going to be made Secretary of the Congregation of the Religious, and Barbara Ward, Secretary of the Congregation of the Laity. I also am going to ask Bishop Butler if he'll head up a new office combining all our relationships with other religions, and I think Cardinal Suenens will make a great Secretary of State, if I can ever persuade him to leave Belgium. Also, we're going to need a man like Cardinal Cody to straighten out the financial mess around here. Beyond that, I am consulting with some of my closest advisers to find out what other talent is available that we might be able to recruit to serve in the

cabinet. I hope to have more specific announcements in a week
or two, but you've got to realize that this whole thing has taken
me somewhat by surprise.

Q. (*Wall Street Journal*) Are we to take it, sir, that you are going
to make public the financial status of the Vatican?

A. Well, I'm going to try and do it as soon as I can figure out what
the financial status is. As far as I can understand, nobody but
God exactly understands the finances of the Vatican, and unfortunately he's not about to make a private revelation on the
subject.

Q. (*Triumph*) Most Holy Father—

A. I'm not Holy, and I'm certainly not Most Holy, and I'm also
certainly not your father or anybody else's, so call me Pope,
or Mr. Pope, or Bishop, and drop the rest of that nonsense.

Q. (*Triumph*, again) You will, of course, maintain the papal diplomatic service?

A. I will most certainly do no such thing. The only reason we ever
had diplomatic service in the first place was that communica-
tions weren't very good and they had to have somebody on the
scene who could make decisions in the name of the Papacy.
Given the kind of communication we have now, the diplomatic
service is obsolescent, so it seems to me that the first thing we
do is to transfer all the powers of the nuncios and the apostolic
delegates to the National Conference of Bishops. Then they
should send representatives to Rome to deal with the central
offices here. There's no point in running the Church as though
the jet airplane and the radiotelephone hadn't been invented.

Q. (*National Catholic Reporter*) What contribution, if any, do you
think the lay people have to make to the life of the Church?

A. What contribution, if any? Well, that's kind of a silly question;
they don't have any *contribution* to make—they *are* the Church.
Without them we might just as well fold up our tents and steal
away into the hills, if only because without them nobody is going
to pay to keep the organization going. As a matter of fact, given
the way we've treated the lay people for so long, I am surprised

that they have paid as much as they have to keep us going. We shouldn't make any major decisions, it seems to me, until the implications of these decisions have been kicked around at the grass roots and we've got the reaction of the rank-and-file membership to what's going on. So we've got to have an assembly of the lay people of the parish and of the diocese and of the national churches, and then finally, of the international Church. As soon as we can possibly get this sort of thing set up, we're going to do it. The trouble is that we can't do it overnight, so we're going to have to limp along for a while without having the advantage of grass-roots participation. But one of the first things I intend to toss into the laps of my colleagues when I get together with the Synod is the problem of how we can most quickly get an international network of lay senates established. If we don't have them, we are certainly going to make the Holy Spirit work overtime.

Q. (Los Angeles *Times*) Do you expect, sir, that there is going to be much change in the canon law in the near future?

A. You better believe there are going to be changes. I have the highest respect for the code of the canon law; it is one of the greatest legal masterpieces of all time, and that's why I think we must let it be a living masterpiece and evolve into something that's even more perfect than itself. Of course its evolution is going to be rather dramatic, I think, in years to come, because very clearly what we need is some sort of international constitution which sets down general principles, and particularly, general rights and freedoms, and then lets the local hierarchies worry about legislating to meet their own problems.

Q. (St. Louis *Post-Dispatch*) Do you expect to separate the legislative and judicial functions of the Church?

A. Oh, you almost have to do that, if you're going to keep everybody honest. It seems to me that we ought to turn the Roman Rota into a kind of supreme court of the Church, to which people can appeal when they feel that their rights have been violated by the lower courts; and the exact shape of the lower courts should be determined by each national hierarchy. Given the complexity of the world today, it would be a terrible burden on the Roman judges to expect them to understand the problems that come in from every country, so they really should only have to hear the most important kind of appellate cases.

Q. (Detroit *Free Press*) Does that mean, sir, that you intend to have a reform of marriage legislation?

A. I almost wish you hadn't asked that, because that's one of the most fouled-up problems that we have to face. I've got some of my staff working already on some temporary changes that are going to improve on the methods we're already using. I certainly hope that somebody in the Synod of Bishops has a brilliant idea of how we can straighten the mess out permanently, but I, for one, am at a loss as to how to do it. Nevertheless, I think we ought to get out of the divorce-trial business. It just seems to me that the Church would have been better off long ago if all the people we've trained to be canon lawyers had been trained to be counseling psychologists instead.

Q. (*Figaro* of Paris) Do you plan, sir, to have any more papal trips?

A. Well, I like to travel as much as the next man, and maybe even a little more. But it seems to me that traveling is more of a vacation than anything else, and I don't expect to learn much on my trips. If the national hierarchies elect good leaders, I presume they'll be the ones who will keep me informed on what's going on, but it seems to me that the papal trip really is pretty much a waste of time. Just the same, let me assure you I'm not going to spend the rest of my term in Rome.

Q. (Manchester *Guardian*) What do you intend to do about *Osservatore Romano*?

A. I wish to heaven I knew what to do about it—would you like to be editor of it?

Q. No, sir, I wouldn't.

A. Yeah, that's what they all say. Next question, please.

Q. (New Orleans *Times-Picayune*) What is your position on the celibacy question?

A. Well, it's pretty clear we've got to do something about it, though I don't want to be stampeded into it until we give the Synod and the various priest and lay senates around the world the time to talk about it. I think we ought to make it easy for people to get out of the priesthood who want to with the promise that, if we do decide to have a married priesthood, we'll give them the option of getting back in—although I think we're going to want to take the option of not letting them back in under some circumstances. You know, every once in a while I'm inclined to think we should let anybody leave the priesthood who wants to, just so long as they and the women they're going to marry are ready to undergo a year of psychotherapy. But I don't suppose you could impose that any more—that might be too autocratic. Just the same, it might be nice if we made the therapy available for them; we would also probably run out of psychiatrists.

Q. (Frankfurter *Zeitung*) Do you expect there to be any heresy trials in your administration?

A. Good God, no!

Q. (Frankfurter *Zeitung*) But what is your opinion of heresy?

A. Well, I don't know that I can find much trace in the Bible of the idea that there was such a thing as heresy—it seems to me to be an idea that came along much later on, and I wonder if we might not be well advised to put it aside. I think there may well be some theologians who speak a little bit beyond what the consciousness of the Church's own message would be able to permit, at the present time; but I'd much prefer to handle this by having a board of theologians sit down and discuss the matter with the theologian who seems to have gone beyond the consciousness and see whether it can be worked out—see whether he really can say the things he says and still, at least at the present time, be part of us. But the idea of excommunicating people and labeling them heretics seems to me to be terribly old-fashioned.

Q. (Frankfurter *Zeitung*) But what do you think of the case of
Reverend Dr. Hans Küng?

A. You mean do I think Hans is a heretic? Why, don't be silly.
Hans is basically a conservative. I never could understand why
people thought he was dangerous or a radical. How in the world
can anybody who owns an Alfa-Romeo be a radical?

Q. (*Il Messaggero*) What, your Holiness—I mean, Pope—what is
your opinion on the forthcoming Italian elections?

A. I hope everybody votes in them.

Q. (*Il Messaggero*) But what party are you supporting?

A. We've got a secret ballot in this country just like most other
countries and who I vote for is my secret.

Q. (*Il Messaggero*) But are you going to take a stand in Italian
politics?

A. What's the matter? Do you think I'm crazy?

Q. (*Il Messaggero*) Does this mean, then, that the Vatican is
assuming a policy of non-intervention in Italian politics?

A. You bet your life it does.

Q. (Milwaukee *Sentinel*) Do you intend, sir, to continue the practice of censorship of books that are written by Catholics?

A. I think it would be a good idea to take every imprimatur in
the world and throw it in the furnace, and we ought to throw
half of the book censors in the furnace, too. The basic thing to
say about censorship is that it didn't work, it doesn't work,
and it's never going to work, and the quicker we forget about it,
the better off we're all going to be.

Q. (Washington *Post*) From all you've said so far, sir, it would
seem that you are really anticipating a very notable decline in
papal authority. I wonder if you could tell us whether you think
that this is a drastic change in Church doctrine?

A. Well, I don't know where you got that idea; I must say, as a
matter of fact, I think what I'm talking about is a rather notable
increase in papal authority. A pope who is informed by his colleagues in the Synod and by the lay people of the world and a
network of lay associations, who has had for his advisers the best

theologians and scholars in the world, who makes informed decisions and can rely on co-operation with these decisions, isn't exactly a weak leader. On the contrary, I think he's a pretty strong one. It's not my intention to weaken the powers of the Papacy at all, but to strengthen the powers of the Papacy, and the reforms that I've discussed are designed to do just that. I might also say that it's probably going to increase the work of the Papacy, and that's why I don't intend to spend much more than five or ten years in the office. You know, it's kind of easy to make unilateral decisions, but it's awfully hard to gain consensus.

Q. (Philadelphia *Inquirer*) Do you mean, then, that you view the Papacy as being essentially a role of one who presides over a consensus?

A. Well, it depends on what you mean by presides. If you mean, do I just sit back and wait until everybody's ideas come in and then co-ordinate them, I can assure you that's not how I intend to play the part. But if you mean, am I going to provide the answers to questions, then let me tell you that things aren't going to be that way at all. It seems to me that the most important job of a man in my position is not to answer questions, but to ask them; not to provide people with answers, but to challenge them to find out what the answers are. That's going to be a pretty tough job, and I'm going to have to gather some of the best minds in the world around me if I'm going to be able to pull it off.

Q. (NBC News) Do you think, sir, that your job as Sovereign Pontiff is going to be a difficult one?

A. Sovereign Pontiff! The trouble with you, David is that you've been reading *Osservatore Romano* too much. Sure, it's going to be a difficult job. Any top-level administrative job is difficult, but if you surround yourself with a good staff and make sure the channels of communication are open, it's not an impossible job. As I say, I think ten years is plenty in it, but I'm rather looking forward to it.

Q. (*Le Monde*) What do you think about the conflict between science and religion?

A. I don't think there is one, and if there has been one, we'll now put a stop to it.

Q. (CBS News) Do you have any opinion, sir, on the question of the emerging nations?

A. Well, I'm certainly going to support the encyclicals on the subject written by my predecessors, though I don't think I'm going to issue any new encyclicals—as a matter of fact, I think we probably ought to declare a moratorium on encyclical writing. I'm going to wait until we get the Synod together and see what my colleagues from these nations think would be the best policy for the Church to assume in the matter. Given the immense number of people that we have in many of these nations, it seems to me that we ought to be doing a much better job than we are. I have a hunch that there might be something wrong with the leadership the Church is providing in the new nations, and if there is, you can believe that there's going to be a real shake-up.

Q. (Miami *Herald*) Do you think the religious life of the priests and brothers and sisters is going to survive?

A. Well, it's not going to survive unless a lot of religious communities get a move on and take themselves out of the Middle Ages. Those who are willing to modernize, democratize, and treat the members like human beings, I think have a great future ahead of them. This is a day when everybody is crying for community, and a good religious order should be able to provide more community than anything else. But my personal opinion is that a lot of them are so bad that they simply are beyond redemption. That's one of the problems that my colleagues in the Synod are going to have to work out, too.

You know, there's something I'd like to say to you fellows. These questions have all been pretty good, but they're mostly on the internal problems of the Church. I suppose I can understand why you'd ask them, because most of the news the Church has made in the last coupla hundred years has had to do with internal problems. We were bogged down for so long in ancient morbid structures that I guess the modernization of these structures was news. But I think I can tell you that by a year from now, or two years at the most, we're going to be so modernized that all you'll be able to ask me is about substantive questions, like— What has the Church got to say about the meaning of human love? or What does it have to say about the quest for freedom? or What does it have to say about life and death? What does it have to say about getting old? or about leisure? or about the mass media? I'm kinda glad you're not asking me those questions now, because I haven't the faintest idea what the answers are, and I can't even promise that I'll have very good answers a year from now, but they're going to be better than the present ones. Any more questions?

Q. (*Seventeen*) Do you have anything to say for young people?

A. Well, I'd say to the young to be patient with us older people because we're going to try and learn how to listen to you, and that we'll try, in our turn, to be patient with you while you try to learn how to listen to us. I don't think there's much wrong with young people that a little bit of experience won't cure— and there's not much wrong with older people that sharing the enthusiasm of the young won't cure.

Q. (New York *Times*) Thank you, Mr. Pope.

A. You're quite welcome, Scotty.

Conclusion

The 1960s were a decade in which human emotions were rediscovered, but it is too early to say what the rediscovery means. Is the mind-blowing with which this book is concerned merely a lamentable transient accident, or does it rather represent the wave of the future? Are we going to integrate emotions into the human intellectual life, or are we going to abandon the intellect? Are we moving into an age of generosity, or narcissism; of peacemakers, or polarizers? Is ours the time of the rediscovery of the sacred and transcendent, or of the destruction of civility and rationality? Do we live in a period when moral enthusiasm has been rediscovered, or rather a period when bigotry and intolerance have definitively reasserted themselves? Is John Kennedy the symbol of our times, or Timothy Leary? Is it Robert Kennedy or Herbert Marcuse who will be most remembered a hundred years from now? Does Martin Luther King represent the thrust of the black people, or does Eldridge Cleaver? Does Cletus O'Donnell or James Shannon point the way for liberal young bishops? Does John XXIII or James Kavanaugh represent future Christianity? Is Karl Rahner the man for our times, or rather must we look for the future to the smart-aleck young columnist of the *National*

Catholic Reporter who did not think that Karl Rahner ought to be a priest? Does a relatively conservative theologian such as Hans Küng represent the Church's witness in the twentieth century, or does the executive officer of the National Association of Laymen shouting obscenities at a bishops' meeting and then justifying these obscenities on the grounds that they were "black language"? Is Dan Herr the typical Catholic journalist in the modern world, or is Peter Steinfels? Will we look for leadership to those who think it a peak religious experience to talk in foreign tongues, or rather to those who proclaim the good news in language that is pertinent to a world more desperately searching for meaning than ever before? Ought we respect more the clergy who are desperately laboring to build a new Church, or those who are desperately trying to pull down the old one? Do we conclude that the self-actualized clergy are the ones who get out, or are they the ones who stay and fight?

There is not much doubt, I am sure, in the reader's mind with which side I would line up, but I am not at all sure that that is going to be the winning side. On the contrary, I am more prepared than I have ever been in my life to accept the fact that the things that I stand for represent the losing side, at least in the short run. In the long run, I am sure that the power of the Holy Spirit (speaking in English) and the power of human reason are both such that the mind blowers and the reactionaries will be swept from the field. But as Lord Keynes said in his incisive remark, "In the long run, we'll all be dead."

And yet, the long run may not be all that long. It seems to me that those of us who try to combine affect and intellect, rationality and mythology, reason and the spirit, are in fact, in an age of romanticism, the most romantic people of all. The mind blowers, the anti-intellectuals, the romanticists are not embarked on an adventure; they are rather engaging in a childish tantrum. As G. K. Chesterton pointed out so long ago, orthodoxy is the real adventure. Both reason and emotion, instead of reason or emotion; both structure and spirit, instead of either structure or spirit; both tradition and future, instead of either tradition or future. How many adventurers like Chesterton remain in the American Church is not clear at the present moment, but if there are enough of them, the mind blowers will be a temporary aberration.